M000084970

"In this affecting, evocative memoir, Professor Chitpin recounts her extraordinary childhood, growing up as an orphan in the Fook Soo Am Buddhist Pagoda at the end of a dirt road in Mauritius. As she traces the people and events of her life up until her first years as a student in Canada, important themes emerge. We see the complexity of human identity, different kinds of family bonds, the significance of education, and the challenges of moving across and between cultures. Professor Chitpin, now an established academic, also exposes the fragility of our lives and shows how for many children from disadvantaged backgrounds, there is no easy path to success." Richard Barwell, Professor and Dean, Faculty of Education, University of Ottawa

"More than a life course, Stephanie Chitpin's book fits in the landscape of Mauritian autobiographical texts as a 'quest.' It is the reflection of a deep and permanent search aimed at filling a void and providing answers to one of the greatest philosophical questions that one can put to oneself: who am I?

"Her story gives us above all a lesson of courage and perseverance in the face of adversity, whatever form it may choose to take in one's life. One can see in the journey of this orphan girl who grew up in the heart of Port-Louis, capital of Mauritius, while being somehow excluded from it, whose family was limited to a community of sisters in a pagoda, and whose connections outside the pagoda were confined to one or two families of Mauritian-Chinese traders, an enormous and unusual strength of character." Professor Arnaud Carpooran, Dean, Faculty of Social Sciences and Humanities, University of Mauritius

KEEP MY MEMORY SAFE

KEEP MY MEMORY SAFE
Fook Soo Am, The Pagoda

A Memoir by
STEPHANIE CHITPIN

Baraka
Books

Montréal

All rights reserved. No part of this book may be reproduced or transmitted in any form or by any means, electronic or mechanical, including photocopying, recording, or by any information storage and retrieval system, without permission in writing from the publisher.

© Stephanie Chitpin

ISBN 978-1-77186-316-2 pbk; 978-1-77186-324-7 epub; 978-1-77186-325-4 pdf

Cover and Book Design by Folio infographie
Editing and proofreading: Blossom Thom, Anne Marie Marko, Daniel J. Rowe

Legal Deposit, 2nd quarter 2023
Bibliothèque et Archives nationales du Québec
Library and Archives Canada

Published by Baraka Books of Montreal

Printed and bound in Quebec

TRADE DISTRIBUTION & RETURNS

Canada – UTP Distribution: UTPdistribution.com

United States
Independent Publishers Group: IPGbook.com

We acknowledge the support from the Société de développement des entreprises culturelles (SODEC) and the Government of Quebec tax credit for book publishing administered by SODEC.

Société
de développement
des entreprises
culturelles
Québec

Funded by the Government of Canada
nancé par le gouvernement du Canada | Canada

CONTENTS

Dedicated to the memory of
Ah Feeti of Fook Soo Am
for all her love, care and dedication.

FOREWORD

Professor Stephanie Chitpin shares with such integrity and openness her life journey that, as a privileged reader, I am filled with gratitude. My spontaneous feedback to Professor Chitpin over the phone was, "You are so brave!" We do not choose how and where we come into this world; Professor Chitpin confronts with lucidity the circumstances surrounding her birth, her early years and the subsequent arch of her trajectory. The narrative is delightful, at times tinged with a poignant undertone but always upbeat.

Following the first reading of this fascinating memoir, I had a visual experience. It was like contemplating a tapestry woven intricately and presenting the picture of a mountain climbing adventure. The main character of this picture/adventure is a lone climber secured however by *"la cordée"* (the rope team) made up of numerous *"gui ren"* (proverbial term in Chinese meaning the benefactor/helper/savior encountered by chance along the way). The constants in the picture are the climber and the physical rope, which I envision as a golden thread. The multiple *"gui ren"* join the *"cordée,"* attracted by the golden thread which, to me, illustrates the determination and intelligence of the climber. It is not a smooth and glorious ascent, there are episodes of "broken hearts" because difficult choices had to be taken at crossroads. However, a laser focus keeps the climber sure-footed however rough the terrain. Along the way the climber draws her own conclusions about life:

> "Often, we discover the place in us that carries the light only after it has become dark. Sometimes it is only in the dark that we know the value of this place" (105).

Besides being an inspirational true story, the memoir saves from oblivion historical facts about the founding of Fook Soo Am and life in Chinatown in Rue Leoville L'Homme in the '70s. Mr. Chui's teashop activities, remembered vividly with love, enable many of us to relive with nostalgia our own past experience as immigrants or children of Chinese immigrants.

The title *Keep My Memory Safe: Fook Soo Am, The Pagoda* is a fortunate choice because this sanctuary had shaped the life not only of Professor Chitpin but of a multitude of Chinese people, as well as other communities, anchoring each supplicant in his/her Faith in Buddha or Pow Koung or Guan Yin. Ah Feeti's call in the founding of Fook Soo Am introduces us to the realm of Mystery.

"Mystery came to occupy a central place in my life" (153), writes Professor Chitpin. Does not Mystery envelope the story? I tend to believe that somewhere there is a superb organizer who provided the overall structure within which "the mountain climber" could thrive and be nudged along. The author cited Dr. Rachel Ramen: "By its very nature, a Mystery cannot be solved; it can never be known. It can only be lived" (151).

The Mystery is also lived by Ah Feeti, the foundress of Fook Soo Am, who feels her powerlessness in the last days of her life of service to a sacred cause. It reminds us of Jesus's words, as recorded in the Gospel: "So you also, when you have done everything you were told to do, should say, 'we are unworthy servants; we have only done our duty'" (Luke 17:10). Such is the ultimate *"détachement"* (renunciation), a cold fact of life, experienced by many founders of religious institutions; by the way it could also be the plight awaiting many of us at the end of our earthly itinerary, couldn't it?

Some lessons learned: Mr. Chui's firm belief in education (a trait of our Hakka DNA) and extraordinary generosity, Hannah's and Koung Koung's unconditional nurturing care and Ah Pak's daring initiative to raise a child, plus the dedication of many other *"gui ren"* have achieved beyond expectation what each one could have dreamed of concerning their protégée. SOLIDARITY, another saving grace in the Sino-Mauritian community around education, made it all possible.

It is not lost on Professor Chitpin, who takes over the leadership of a new *"cordée"* (rope team), as we learn in her acknowledgements (169), "In 2021, I created a scholarship at the University of Ottawa in Ah Pak's name: the Ah Feeti of Fook Soo Am Memorial Scholarship. Through this I hope to help racialized students, including Indigenous, Métis and Inuit, who are pursuing undergraduate degrees in the Faculty of Education." Thank you, Professor Chitpin, for showing the way to young and old! There might be a *"cordée"* out there beckoning us!

Sister Cécile Leung, Ph. D (University of Chicago),
Professor Emerita, Winthrop University,
South Carolina, USA

PROLOGUE

Many of us are quite average in our lives, even if we are exceptional in one or two things. To become truly great takes time, energy, and dedication. But because we all have limited access to all that, few of us become truly exceptional in anything, and I am no different.

Some would see my background as having been very constrained and my trajectory unexceptional. And yet, it was, and it wasn't. There are those who have led a stable existence in one place, never having ventured far from where they were born. My life, however, was marked by displacement from its very beginning. Sometimes I think that it was my life's very instability that led me so fiercely towards solidity and success.

I am compelled to leave a record of how I was encouraged to see past the many walls and obstacles that surrounded me in the remote island of Mauritius, where I was raised. My beginnings as a child ward of a Buddhist temple, and the lessons I learned from my principal guardians—a head nun and a businessman— have left an indelible mark on me and made me who I am today. Perhaps not great, but certainly striving towards it.

From childhood I wanted an education—not a given for a child in my situation—and as I grew older, I wanted even more, such as to travel abroad and leave my past behind. The process to envision these things, hold fast to that vision, then find ways to make them happen was gruelling and exhausting but, ultimately, extraordinarily rewarding. It also broke my heart in two.

I left Mauritius not because of the values that drive me, or because I had a thirst to discover another world, or even because I was curious to meet other people from other cultures. Rather, it was to escape a haunting outline of shame circumscribing every aspect of my life. This was the shame of being an orphan, of being raised in a temple, and of relying on the kindness and generosity of others. I had no status, and perhaps worse, my status was as an illegitimate child. Very little was expected of me, and I was taught to expect even less.

I was barely aware of it at the time, though I could feel it. When I was teased by classmates or called a bastard, I pretended that I did not understand and that it did not hurt. I did not rationalize it at the time, or process it in any way, but it wounded me and left scars. It fueled my determination and, ultimately, my departure.

Shame has followed me since birth. Being born ashamed of my veiled origins, and shame about my lack of legitimacy in the eyes of the Mauritian state, I learned to create my own sense of self early on. At some point in my youth, I decided to be happy and to be in control of my life. I chose not to picture myself constantly as a victim which, in any case, requires much energy and self-absorption. I never believed that my problems were insurmountable. I understood that I was not alone, that if I have any sort of problem, chances are that scores of other people do as well. Realizing that I am not special is, ironically, what saved me.

And so, I want to share my story. I would like this little volume to be a bridge of sorts between Mauritius and Canada, and between the lives of people whose beginnings are unimaginable to the comfortable citizens of faraway lands. In particular, I wish to send a message to those who still know me back in the old country that I love them and care for them, that I think about them often, and that I hope they will keep my memory safe.

This is a record for my friends in Mauritius of how they have touched my life. And for my friends in Canada, a little window into how my life became what it is today.

Chapter 1

ONE CHILD

Oye. Oi-Chu Shiu Fook Sien. Ah Foong. Seymoye. Stephanie. I have had many names in my life. I answer to them all.

My parents were living in Indonesia, working in a garment factory, when they found out my mother was pregnant. While their circumstances would improve and they would eventually be able to start their own textile business, at the time they could not fathom raising a fifth child. My father knew of Ah Pak, also known as Ah Feeti, a distant cousin living as a Buddhist nun in Mauritius. They made arrangements to meet her in Hong Kong, where my mother was to give birth in a clinic called the Kennedy Club. Ah Pak was to smuggle me out of the country. My mother gave me one thing before handing me over, my name: Oi-Chu Shiu Fook Sien, meaning Love Pearl.

I was only a few days old when Ah Pak transported me in a woven straw basket to a small island off the coast of Africa. When it was time to go through Mauritian customs and immigration, Mr. Chui, a well-respected philanthropist and businessman, used his connections to help me enter the country unofficially. Hence, despite my birth certificate, no papers were ever drawn up for me and the government would never know that I existed.

Two cars full of people drove to meet Ah Pak and the baby at the airport. In one car was Hannah, Ah Pak's friend and confidant, and her youngest boy, Seth, who was nine at the time. The car they were in was involved in an accident on the way to the airport and Seth suffered minor scrapes on both of his legs. Years later, Seth would remind me that he was the first among his siblings to meet me: "And nothing could stop us, not even an accident!!"

After the long and nerve-wracking journey, Ah Pak handed me over to Hannah, who would become my nanny for the next four years.

Hannah lived with her husband, Mr. Li, and their three children, Steve, Seth and Francine in a rental house on Lapaix Street. To reach Hannah's house, you need to climb a set of stairs to the second floor of a big rectangular building, where there were several apartment units.

Hannah shared her double bed with me, and next to us Francine had a single bed beside the wall that separated their bedroom from the kitchen. Hannah had to remind me almost every day not to jump on the beds as the mattresses were made out of straw and would easily disintegrate. I did not like Francine because she was bossy, so when she was at school or when no one was looking, I would jump on her bed. I wanted to see it fall apart, with the pieces of straw scratching her skin. Replacing a mattress would have been a considerable expense for the family at the time. Luckily, my obstinacy did not win out and the mattresses prevailed. Across the hall was the second bedroom that Mr. Li shared with his two sons, Steve and Seth.

Hannah showered me with constant love and affection, perhaps as a bulwark against the constant bickering and criticism meted out by her husband. He did not like her cooking for some reason, always finding fault with the quantity of salt or sugar or soya sauce she used. She in turn berated him for his overly generous use of oil when he cooked on Sundays. Because of this, and that we did not have a television, we children spent all our free time outdoors, as far away from the house as we could, given our age and little legs.

On Sundays, Mr. Li went to the market to buy a live chicken. He brought it home and killed it by slitting the throat and letting it bleed out over the stones. Filled with equal measures of dread and curiosity, I would stand behind Mr. Li and watch him slaughter and then dress the bird. When it was served, the boys got the chicken breasts, thighs and legs and the girls got the bony parts.

Francine resented her parents for favouring her brothers over her, but it was a cultural norm in Mauritius and they didn't think twice about doing it.

When Mr. Li had extra money he would bring home a second chicken and keep it in the coop on the roof of the house. When Seth was older, he was allowed to kill the second chicken by slitting its throat just as he had seen his father do. The first time, the poor animal escaped and ran into the bedroom where I was playing, its head hanging by a single tendon. The frantic bird bounced against the walls in a frenzy, spraying the room with blood, even landing at one point on the bed. I screamed in horror as everyone chased the chicken through the house. It took a long time to clean up the mess. Because of this, I never ate chicken again, and still don't to this day.

Mr. Li was the only breadwinner in the family. He gave Hannah a monthly stipend for food and other essentials. It was supposed to last until his next pay cheque, but it rarely did. Like many women, Hannah played Bian Kim, a Hakka card game, with her friends and relatives. Hosting and attending games cost money, as did the fact that she lost more often than not.

As a result, when Hannah went to the market with Ah Pak to buy fruits and vegetables, Ah Pak would share some of her groceries and would ask the merchants for extra fruits or vegetables for her.

The Li family had dinner between 4:30 and 5 p.m. but by 8 p.m., the children were hungry again. Hannah bought inexpensive and rejected cream crackers in bulk and would feed them to us with some margarine and a cup of tea. It was not the healthiest of snacks, but we avoided going to bed hungry.

After living with the Li family for four years, Ah Pak decided that it was time for me to reside in the temple. My destiny was to be a ward of the pagoda and serve as a novice nun for the rest of my life. It was time to start my training and begin a life of service, scarcity, and sacrifice.

Hannah brought me to the temple with a bag of clothes. I held on to her and did not want her to leave my sight. Ah Pak distracted me with a toy and some candies, until Hannah was able to leave. When I realized she was gone, I cried uncontrollably and called for her for the rest of the day.

Mama, mama, I cried nonstop.

But Ah Pak told me she was not my mother and I should stop thinking about her. Ah Pak was a good person, but she did not know how to deal with children.

For weeks, I suffered severe separation anxiety and cried constantly and threw tantrums. Hannah came back to look in on me several times during this period. Perhaps she missed me as much as I missed her. I clung to her so tightly that I left marks and tore at her dress. It was an exhausting and gruelling roller coaster: ecstatic excitement upon seeing her, followed by inconsolable grief.

Many years later, I wondered if I had been responsible for the demise of Ah Pak and Hannah's relationship. Perhaps Ah Pak was jealous of my connection with Hannah and my insistence that I preferred her food, her clothing, her toys, her presence. When the Li family moved closer to the tea store many years later, I would secretly visit Hannah and we reconnected. I did not tell Ah Pak about these meetings, even then. Any present or toy that Hannah gave me, I hid. It was mine and mine alone.

Chapter 2

THE PAGODA

The pagoda was built in 1954, long before I was born.

When she arrived in Mauritius as a young girl, Ah Pak was taken to serve at a pagoda called Pu Thee Chi. It was not a happy place, she told me, and she witnessed and experienced a great deal of inequity and even some cruelty. It was because of this that she made the decision to build her own pagoda, a temple where all would be treated fairly, regardless of race, sex, and socio-economic status. She eventually befriended one of the visitors to Pu Thee Chi, Hannah Li, who agreed to put her up in their two-bedroom apartment while they waited for donations to build a new pagoda.

With Hannah's help, Ah Pak canvassed door-to-door for donations and managed to get enough money to look for a piece of land on which to build. It was during the canvassing that she met the Chui family. Mr. Chui was known as a credible and generous businessman, and he pledged himself to help her build the pagoda.

One night, as Ah Pak was praying in Hannah's apartment, she saw summer irises on the east side of the grey sky as it rained. The next day, she asked what the name of the neighbourhood was where she saw the summer irises. But neither Hannah nor her husband knew. So, she went to speak with Mr. Chui, who would be out walking every morning. She told him that she had been praying for Buddha to give her some signs as to where she should be looking for a piece of land to build a pagoda and wondered whether the summer irises were a sign.

Mr. Chui told her that she had seen the flowers in Plaine Verte, but it was not a desirable neighbourhood as it was very poor and mostly Muslim (rather than Buddhist). He counselled her to look elsewhere, but Ah Pak kept insisting that Buddha had given her a sign to build the pagoda in Plaine Verte. Unable to convince her otherwise, Mr. Chui contacted a real estate broker.

They looked at a vacant lot not yet on the market but that the owner was contemplating selling. The land was located at the foot of a mountain surrounded by houses mostly built of straw or mud. Mr. Chui was uncomfortable with the idea of helping Ah Pak acquire a piece of land in the middle of nowhere. To get to the foot of the mountain, one had to go through Plaine Verte and through a steep narrow mud road. It was only accessible on foot or by bicycle.

Mr. Chui stalled the process by asking the broker to look for sites in better neighbourhoods. Other locations were suggested, but Ah Pak was not satisfied with any of them. She kept asking Mr. Chui to help her place an offer on the vacant lot by the foot of the mountain, even though it was not for sale. Exhausted, Mr. Chui asked the broker to put an offer on the vacant lot. The offer was rejected by the seller who by that time had changed his mind about selling.

A couple of months passed until one night, Ah Pak said that she had dreamed that Buddha had told her that it was time to place an offer again. She asked Mr. Chui if he could please contact the landowner. Mr. Chui explained that one cannot be forced to sell one's property. Still, she was adamant.

The seller lived with his family in one of the straw houses that would sit just below the pagoda on the narrow mud road. When Mr. Chui finally met with him, he described how the land would be used for a Buddhist temple and that a young nun was wanting to build it. The seller, who was of Buddhist faith, was so moved that he agreed to sell the land to Ah Pak directly without charging broker fees.

It took almost two years to build the pagoda, a modest cement building in the middle of nowhere. It was unusual at the time—and still is—for a single nun without sponsorship to build a Pagoda herself. But through persistence and countless small donations, Ah Pak achieved what few before or after her have done. She built a temple.

According to Francine, the seller acted as *le gardien*, a custodian, during the early years and took no fee for the service. He wanted to ensure that there were no intruders or animals hiding in the bushes and that Ah Pak was safe.

I vaguely remember the seller in the later years of his life. Every time he paid Ah Pak a visit, she would share food the worshippers left, and they would exchange a few words, mostly using signs or body language, as le gardien spoke only Creole, which Ah Pak barely knew how to speak. He reminded me of a homeless man, always wearing the same clothing and going about barefoot. All I know about him is that he was good and decent. I was seven or eight years old when he died. We all went to his funeral. As there was no crematory at that time, his body was laid on top of a pyre made up of firewood. I was scared and remember holding Ah Pak's hand tightly. Ah Pak was crying together with his family.

The finished pagoda— called Fook Soo Am meaning good luck, blessings and longevity and known in the local jargon as the Pagode Chinois—was a simple rectangular structure with cement walls and a corrugated tin roof. From Boulevard Hugon, worshippers follow the steps to the main entrance. Once at the door, there is a walkway of another couple of hundred metres. A large concrete veranda is the first thing you see inside, within which is a large statue of the Buddha, the Bodhisattva. Next to him is Guan Yin, the Goddess of Mercy, the physical embodiment of compassion. She is an all-seeing, all-hearing being who is called upon by worshippers in times of uncertainty, despair, and fear. Her identity was originally based on the Bodhisattva Avalokiteśvara.

A cement wall separates the Buddha and Guan Yin from Pow Koung Low Yah and the other Goddesses. On either side of Pow Koung Low Yah are the two bedrooms—one on the left and one on the right. Further

right is the kitchen, followed by a set of stairs and a
walkway that leads to a smaller building that houses
guests or overnight worshippers from out of town, as
well as volunteers who would stay a day or two to help
the nuns make rice cakes or noodles for the spring
festivals or for the God's or Goddesses' birthday.

Legend had it that, even though the temple was built
in the so-called bad neighbourhood of Plaine Verte, the
Gods being worshipped there will answer your prayers.
Consequently, there were constant visitors and much
incense. So much incense in fact that the smoke was
all-pervading, its scent sticking to hair, clothes, and
memories. There was no ventilation, so the effect was
harsh, and I would wake up every morning with watery
eyes and a runny nose. From seven in the morning to
two in the afternoon or so, the incense was at its peak.
Our lives were very quiet, with every day spent only
working. There was not much conversation going on,
not even a "How was your day?" The only sound you
would be likely to hear was that of the ritual gong and
drum. The Buddha rested in the afternoon, along with
the three dogs that roamed the pagoda courtyard, so
I would have a small break from my flu-like symp-
toms, only to begin again the next day. This worried
Koung Koung, who was Ah Pak's mother superior in
Meixian, China. She would frequently remind me to
take a Panadol, a brand of acetaminophen, to relieve
my watery eyes and runny nose.

Our lifestyle was informed in part by the 1968
Mauritian riots, a series of racially fuelled alterca-
tions in the neighbourhoods of Cité Martial and Plaine

Verte, which occurred when two rival gangs clashed. Twenty-nine people were killed in the ensuing violence and British troops were brought in to help the Mauritian police. All this happened in the backyard of the pagoda. Although the incident preceded my time, we were taught to keep the pagoda's doors locked and not to venture out after sunset, nor were we allowed to linger on the boulevard.

When I turned five, I saw many girls and boys walking to school along the boulevard. I did not go to school at first, nor did the other girls who resided in the pagoda. This fact set us apart from other children.

When I turned eight, Ah Pak's niece, Ah Fi, was born. Her parents, Lily and François, decided to give up their daughter to the pagoda. I had been the youngest in the pagoda for the longest time and, with the arrival of a new baby, I figured that my life would get busier and more hectic. But soon after the baby arrived, Fen was released from her task of washing all the teacups, as she now had to care for the baby.

The teacups became my responsibility. I would go around and collect them on the altars. There were fifty-five in all. I was barely three feet tall and, to get the cups into the sink, I needed to sit on a high chair to wash them. It would take me over an hour to scrub the tea stains from all the cups. At first, I enjoyed washing because I got to play with water. Then, one day, I broke a couple of cups and Ah Pak was unhappy because she needed to replace them, which would probably cost her a fortune. She spoke sternly and slapped me twice on my cheeks. I cried softly at first; then, when no one heard me, cried louder and louder until Koung Koung consoled me. She held me in her arms and asked me to stop crying. She put some ointment on my red cheeks and asked me to be more careful next time if I didn't want to get slapped. To this day, if I must enter a porcelain collectible store, I do not touch anything. The sign, "You break it, you buy it," does not apply to me, as I received my life lesson from the pagoda.

Chapter 3

AH PAK

I loved Ah Pak's story of Siddhartha Gautama, the Buddha who had been a prince in the royal family. When Buddha was twenty-nine years old, he was confronted with the realities of impermanence and suffering. On one occasion, when he went out of his palace, he saw someone who was very ill. The next day, he saw a decrepit old man and on the third day, a dead person. Through this, he realized that there is no such thing as lasting happiness or protection from human sufferings. Perturbed, he went on a spiritual journey in search of lasting happiness, finding it when one morning he walked past a meditating man who sat in deep absorption. When their eyes met, Buddha was mesmerized. It was at that moment that Buddha realized that the perfection he had been seeking resided not outside, but within the mind, and within the self. He had experienced the taste of true and lasting refuge.

I often asked Ah Pak why she left her parents in Meixian, China, to become a nun in Mauritius and if she, too, was searching for lasting happiness. She had been born to a very poor family, she told me. Her father passed away when she was young and she had an older brother who suffered from epilepsy and died, leaving a widow and four young children. After her father's death, Ah Pak was given away to the monastery to become a nun, which was a common practice in China among poor families.

Along with the pagoda, Ah Pak also built something else: a good reputation. She was much respected for her generosity, and sometimes people even compared her to Mother Teresa. Whatever she asked of her Gods was almost certain to be answered. Early every morning, worshippers would be waiting to consult her on matters of all sorts. When she wasn't dividing her time between consulting and praying, she was teaching us scriptures and handing out tasks.

At the beginning, Ah Pak supervised my training and taught me to ask the Gods to forgive the sins I had committed or was about to commit. I mumbled most of my prayers to myself: "Dear Buddha or Guan Yin, thank you for the food or the treats that so-and-so brought us yesterday and I hope that they will bring me some more soon. Please help me learn how to read and write. I don't want Ah Pak to think I am lazy. Please make her like me and not make me work too hard today."

We were only a handful of people living in the pagoda: Ah Pak, Koung Koung, three girls, and three dogs. Lan, Fen and I were there as wards and were expected to become nuns one day.

Lan had been the middle child in a big family. Neither of her parents worked and so they made the decision to give her up to be raised as a nun. Almost ten years older than I, she had been at the pagoda for several years already by the time I came along.

Her parents would visit her from time to time. They lived north of the pagoda, in Terre-Rouge, and had to take a couple of buses. I remembered them as quiet and timid. Her mother would ask me how school was going and what I had learned. If she harboured some resentment that I was offered schooling and not her daughter, she did not show it.

Fen had lost her father when she was two years old. Her mother, Ah Sen, had difficulty conceiving after the birth of her eldest son, Peter, and made a promise to the Buddha that if they had a girl, they would give her up to the pagoda to become a nun. When Fen reached the age of four, her mother, Ah Sen, gave her to Ah Pak. After that, Ah Sen was able to conceive her youngest boy.

Ah Sen lived on Desforges Street, not far from the pagoda and visited her daughter almost every day, helping her with the washing, cleaning, and mopping. Ah Sen was known to cook well, which I could get a taste of when she brought food for Fen. She did not seem to like me when I was young. She did not mistreat me or anything like that, but she would ignore me as if I did not exist. Years later, I often wondered if Ah Sen's treatment of me had to do with the fact that, unlike Lan's mother, Ah Sen was deeply resentful that her daughter was not given half the opportunities I was. It was an unfair situation, and she must have been reminded of it daily.

On an average day, we would see between five and ten worshippers. They were usually older women who had emigrated from Meixian, China, and did not speak Creole. They were nostalgic for their culture and a familiar language and spent their time at the pagoda when their husbands or children were busy at work or school. They would bring us a bottle of oil or a bag of rice, or even fruits and vegetables. They never came empty-handed.

During harvest season, Ah Pak shared her crops with the volunteers, the latter helping with the pickling and canning for the winter season. The volunteers were mostly from out-of-town and would stay a fortnight as they helped the nuns, including making chips or buns to feed the worshippers. I can still smell the crunchy and spicy *gato-awi*. They were so aromatic and delicious that it soon became known that the pagoda made the best taro fritters on the island. People would drive to the pagoda just to sample the taro fritters.

The other signature dish was the handmade noodles. Made of simple ingredients—flour, salt, and water—they were boiled and then tossed in oil and soya sauce. For special occasions, the noodles would be served with *satini*, a sauce of tomato, oil, salt, vinegar, and coriander.

Lan made breakfast every day. This consisted of a bowl of white rice and some vegetables. After breakfast, we would gather at a long table to make votive candles in different shapes: blocks of gold, boats, flowers, and gold sheets. Sometime around midday, Lan would cook again, this time making fried sweets for snacks, or steamed buns stuffed with vegetables.

Lan and I shared one of the more important chores: the placing of the teacups in front of the God and

Goddess on an altar—three, four or five, the number representing how powerful they were—and we would walk around the pagoda with a bucket filled with teacups. When I was old enough to handle hot water, I brewed the jasmine tea and filled the cups myself.

After that, we went to the garden, which was separated from the pagoda by a cement wall. There, I helped Lan water the many rows of fruits and vegetables. She had a green thumb and loved gardening, and everything that she touched grew. She never got upset with me when, instead of taking care of the fruits and vegetables, I played with the water and got myself wet. She told me to go back to the pagoda to change my clothes and dry myself before Ah Pak saw me, or I would be punished. Some days, I would listen to Lan; other days, I would do whatever suited my fancy.

Once every couple of months, Ah Pak would go to Chinatown and buy incense and gold papers. We would put small quantities of the incense into little bags and sell them to the worshippers at a slightly higher price to cover the transportation cost and to have enough money to feed us. We turned the gold papers into blocks of gold and sold them as votives. The bigger sheets of gold would be used as wrapping paper for boxes filled with money that we made as offerings. The worshippers bought these votives and offered them to different Gods and Goddesses.

We cleaned our workstation around 5 p.m., and I would be reminded that it was time for me to read the Buddhist scripture and practice the chants while Lan prepared dinner. Fen collected the teacups on the altars and washed them, readying them for use the following morning. After dinner, we gathered around the table and Ah Pak taught us scriptures and chants. We repeated the scripture line by line for an hour or two, depending on Ah Pak's mood, until it was time for bed.

It was a treat whenever our duties compelled us to leave the confines of the pagoda and go to town. The cheapest and most frequently used means of transportation was to take the bus, the United Bus Service, commonly referred to as Tip Top. In those years, the roads on the island were mostly unpaved. It took at least an hour to travel by bus from the pagoda to Chinatown and the business district, and the rides were rough. But it was an exciting change of scenery for a small child.

On the morning of our trip, I would get impatient. I remember the indescribable feeling of longing to connect with the real world that I saw only in glimpses: the Chuis, their employees, and other merchants and pedlars. I wanted to know what and how they were doing. I yearned for the feeling of knowing that I was accepted just the way I was and not just seen as a poor orphan girl.

We did our groceries once a month by taxi. Not quite a taxi company, but two men who owned cars and would hire themselves out to take us on our trips. Our favourite taxi driver was Ah Vee Ko, a thin man in his sixties with a calm and polite voice. His clothing was usually coloured in earth tones, often matching his dark brown Volkswagen Beetle. I still remember the licence plate: AF 404. Once a month, he drove Ah Pak to town to stock up on supplies. Since I was the youngest at the pagoda, I was tasked with accompanying Ah Pak to town. I enjoyed riding in the dark Beetle and looked forward to it. Most of the time, it would take us to town without incidents. Every now and then, our day would be hijacked by the battery failing or some other mechanical problem. I can still remember Ah Pak scolding Ah Vee Ko to take care of his car properly so that we would not be stuck on the streets.

When Ah Vee Ko was unavailable, we would hire Mr. Fred. Mr. Fred, who was half-Chinese and half-Mauritian, looked younger than Ah Vee Ko and was probably in his fifties. He was tall and always wore a white shirt, black pants, and black shoes. He noisily sucked air through his mouth every few minutes, which drove me crazy. When Mr. Fred was not driving, he sold cigarettes, soft drinks, and pickled fruit and vegetables from a small convenience store not far from Mr. Chiu's tea shop. He drove a big red 1950s Ford Fairlane, with his right arm hanging on the outside of the driver's door. I disliked riding in Mr. Fred's car. Every time we made a stop, he would take out his rag and clean everything, starting with the roof. He would make us wait until he was satisfied that the car was spotless and gleaming. He drove well below the speed limit to save gas—but also, I was sure, to attract attention from the passersby.

He charged Ah Pak by the hour and so the slower he went, the more money he put in his pocket. He constantly reminded me not to put my fingers on the windows and to keep his car clean. As I got older, I talked back to him when Ah Pak was not watching. I would tell him that he was paid to drive us and not to have us sit in his car watching him clean it. One day, when I was five years old, I told Mr. Fred that he had the ugliest car in the whole wide world, that I was embarrassed to ride in it, and that I would rather take the Tip Top.

This did not go well. He reported me to Ah Pak, who grounded me for a long time. I might have also gotten the strap, but I am not sure. If I did not, it was most likely because Ah Pak agreed that Mr. Fred was taking advantage of our generosity by driving well below the speed limit and making us wait whenever he decided his car needed buffing.

But when Ah Vee Ko was available to drive us, the day would go quite differently. The minute I spotted the taxi, I shouted out, "Get ready! Ah Vee Ko is here!" I ran down the stairs to the front door of the pagoda and Ah Vee Ko would let me in the car while we waited for Ah Pak to join us.

Our first stop was always Mr. Chui's tea store, as it was in the centre of Port Louis in the middle of Chinatown. Once inside, Ah Pak would exchange pleasantries with Mr. and Mrs. Chui and one of their older daughters, Shu, her husband Heng, and their youngest boys, Park and Hu, who worked with their father in the tea store.

For Ah Pak, Mr. Chui was more than just a source of tea. She would show him all the bills that she had received in the mail and ask for his help with reading and paying them. Ah Pak's education in China never went beyond grade three, and she did not read or write French or English. She relied completely on the generosity of Mr. Chui to help her with running the pagoda. She eventually learned a bit of Creole but not enough to be conversant.

When the consultation was over, instead of continuing store-to-store with Ah Pak, I would beg to stay in Mr. Chui's store. Eventually, I began to help him by serving customers who came to buy tea. Many of them assumed I was Mr. Chui's daughter or grand-daughter, and I commanded respect when I asked his employees to carry or get the tea boxes for me when I could not reach them. I spent at least three to four hours in the store while Ah Pak was busy buying supplies. Mr. Chui's family gave me sweets or cakes of all sorts. I was spoiled and for a moment or two, forgot I was an orphan.

Because the site of the pagoda was remote and vulnerable, Hannah would bring her children, Steve, Francine and Seth, to sleep over, in order to keep Ah Pak safe and keep her company from Friday after school until Monday morning. The Li family lived on rue Léoville L'Homme, the same street as Mr. Chui's tea store.

Steve was nine or ten years old. He was studious, bright and sportive, and had a gift with words to express his desires. Growing up, he was the favourite of the family because he was always kind and gentle towards others. When he was not studying, he would babysit me while his mother was preparing meals or out running errands with Ah Pak. The family called me Oye, which was short for Oi-chu, my given name. The three siblings would take turns feeding me or changing my diapers.

According to Francine, who was a couple of years younger than Steve, I was a good baby, only crying when I needed to be fed or to be changed. Unlike her brother Steve, Francine was reserved and liked to spend her time alone with her books. She harboured some resentment towards her parents, who favoured the boys over her and would call on her to do most of the household chores while her two brothers played or studied. Seth was three years younger than Francine and was also quiet. Like his siblings, he loved sports of all kinds, particularly tennis and soccer. He got along well with both of his siblings.

Years later, on a return visit, Francine reminded me that there was no electricity in the pagoda at that time as the electrical company had yet to reach this remote area. Hannah, her mother, and Ah Pak had to cook the evening meal while there was still daylight. The kids would use candlesticks to do their homework.

"Mum would drag all three of us to stay at the pagoda after school on Friday to keep the nuns company and to keep them safe," she recollected. "The pagoda was in the middle of nowhere and Ah Pak was a young nun, and my mum and Mr. Chui did not find it safe to let her stay overnight by herself."

It was a surprise to hear Ah Pak described as "young," but I suppose she must have been. To me, she was older than old, timeless and almost ancient. But seeing her in this new light—a young nun who likely needed more help than she ever received—shifted my awareness around a new corner. I suddenly wondered what these experiences were like for Francine.

I asked her if she and her brothers enjoyed spending weekends at the pagoda.

"Not really," she laughed. "We had to eat vegetarian food, for one thing. And when it rained it got very muddy and dirty inside the pagoda. The mud road would come inside the house."

"What did your father think about his wife and kids sleeping in the pagoda every weekend?"

"Good question," Francine said. "We were too young to know what he thought of mom's decision. But our mom had a strong will. When she decided to do something, she acted on it whether dad liked it or not."

Hannah and Ah Pak had much in common.

Chapter 4

KOUNG KOUNG AND OTHERS

Koung Koung was in her late 60s when she arrived in Mauritius, brought from China by Ah Pak to assist with the daily operations of the pagoda. Together, she and Ah Pak got the garden and orchard going to such an extent that the pagoda was able to almost be self-sufficient. For almost everything else, they relied on donations. They went door-to-door for contributions, sometimes accompanied by Hannah, who was a little bit more fluent in creole. Some would give money, others would give food items such as oil and rice, and still others would volunteer their time working in the garden to get the earth ready for corn, cabbages, chayote, potatoes, beans, and mustard greens.

Koung Koung stood slightly over five feet tall and had long white hair which she was not allowed to cut. I remember it laden with coconut oil and worn in a bun. She wore a black kimono top with a pair of black pants, the standard uniform of the nuns of this order. She was mild-mannered and did not understand a word of Mauritian Creole, speaking only Hakka Chinese.

Ah Pak had helped her emigrate to Mauritius from Meixian, China, where Koung Koung had been her superior.

Perhaps due to the change in dynamics between them, resulting from the fact that Ah Pak was now the mother superior of the pagoda, they were often at odds with each other. They would disagree over various matters and Koung Koung would give Ah Pak the silent treatment while seething with rage. I often tried to calm her down, telling her that what they were arguing over was no big deal. It rarely worked, but the tension would eventually dissipate, and all would be well until the next spat.

I developed a sort of co-dependency with Koung Koung. Her bedroom was next to the kitchen, and I liked visiting her room, where she would show me her collection of small gifts that she had received from worshippers on different occasions, such as the spring festival or the Buddha's or God Pow Koung Low Yah's birthday.

Once, I asked her about Pow Koung Low Yah. I was afraid of him as he appeared very serious, and every time I passed his picture I looked away. She told me that he had been a Chinese politician during the reign of Emperor Renzong, in China's Song Dynasty. He had been known for demonstrating extreme honesty and uprightness, such as sentencing his own uncle for a crime he committed. He had also impeached an uncle of the Emperor Renzong's favourite concubine and had punished powerful families. He was appointed prefect of Song's capital Kaifeng from 1057 to 1058. As a prefect, he had initiated several changes to better hear the grievances of the people, which made him a legendary figure. During his years in office, he gained the honorific title Justice Pow for helping peasants overcome corruption.

Pow Koung Low Yah was a symbol of justice in Chinese society, Koung Koung told me, and that was why so many worshippers came to ask for his help in solving problems and seeking justice. He was one of the most popular Gods in the pagoda. Once I learned this, I would kneel down next to the picture and ask for his help when I was being treated unfairly at school by classmates or teachers.

Every first and fifteenth day of the Lunar calendar, as part of a Buddhist ritual, many worshippers visited the pagoda before they headed out for work to offer incense to Buddha, Guan Yin and Pow Koung Low Yah. On these mornings, Koung Koung would get up an hour earlier and make herself a cup of Chinese tea and ask me to join her. We did not have teacups or granulated sugar or honey. Instead, she poured the tea directly into a drinking glass. I was always afraid that the glass would break, as it was very thin.

Koung Koung did not drink her tea in the same way as the other nuns or anyone else I knew. She would put a piece of rock sugar between her teeth and then drink the hot tea straight from her glass. I picked up the habit and to this day I much prefer drinking tea with a little piece of sugar in my mouth.

After we had finished our tea, she would light some incense. She would have a word with Pow Koung Low

Yah in Hakka, sometimes out loud but mostly she would close her eyes and be quiet. I would stand beside her and wait patiently.

When she finished talking to Pow Koung Low Yah, she would turn to me and rest her hands lightly on the top of my head. She would begin by thanking Pow Koung Low Yah for me and mention my struggles of that week and tell Pow Koung Low Yah something about me that was true and good. Every fortnight I waited for that prayer, curious to find out what it was. If I had made mistakes during these two weeks, she would mention my honesty in telling the truth. If I had failed, she would let Pow Koung Low Yah know how hard I had tried. The few times I had been helpful instead of mischievous, she made sure Pow Koung Low Yah knew, and she asked Him to bless me and to watch over me. These few moments were the only times when I felt completely safe and at rest.

Koung Koung's dream was to save enough money so she could return to Meixian one day and take gifts to her family. Although I grew closer to her as the years passed, she never told me much about her immediate family.

In my teenage years, I shared the bedroom next to the kitchen with her. I slept on a small bed while she took the large double bed. One night, I told her that I might soon be leaving the pagoda for Toronto, Canada. Holding back her tears, she said she was very happy for me but would miss me very much. She reached for the key to the trunk at the foot of her bed and pulled out a rag bag. There were 3,000 French francs inside that she had been saving for her family. She motioned for me to take it because now I was her family, she said. When I refused Koung Koung's money, she insisted until I could not say no any longer. She died a few years later and I never got a chance to say goodbye.

Chapter 5

SCHOOL!

Rumours swirled that I was Ah Pak's daughter. That she had gone to Hong Kong to give birth to me and returned to Mauritius with a baby girl. Things only intensified when she made the decision to send me to school.

It had been Mr. Chui who first suggested it to her. I was bright, he said, and it couldn't hurt for me to get an education. Besides, I'd be able to help out more if I knew more than just Hakka and if I could properly read and write.

Ah Pak may have been resistant at first, but I came to understand that on some level it was an idea she embraced. She valued education very much, even more so that she had not been given the opportunity beyond grade three schooling in China. Despite this, she was extremely intelligent and resourceful. I like to think that she saw something of herself in me.

Yet she struggled with what she saw as the negative consequence of an education: we would leave the pagoda. An education would open many doors, giving us countless reasons and opportunities to seek a life elsewhere. After all, all the girls' parents decided that they were to become nuns. The choice was made for them and not by them. It was always at the back of Ah Pak's mind that if we were educated, we would leave.

In any case, shortly after I turned six years old, Mr. Chui spoke to Ah Pak about sending me to a Western school. He was not a large man, but he was able to command an entire country as far as I was concerned. He had a presence about him and the solemnity of an oracle. His hands were firm but soft, the hands of a man who sat on a leather chair all his life, giving commands to his wife, children, employees, and even government officials. Like Ah Pak, and like Hannah, he was a man who saw what needed to be done and did it. I was enrolled in a one-room kindergarten just up the street from the temple. Mr. Chui paid the one rupee (approximately five Canadian cents) a month for my schooling.

I was the oldest student in that class, as kindergarten starts at age four and I had already missed two years. But I learned Creole with the other students, as well as how to read and write the alphabet. I would show off my newly acquired language and skills to Lan and Fen at the end of the day. By that time, dinner had come and, often, the teacups were washed and dried by either Lan or Fen. I don't remember if the three of us ever fought. But I know now that Ah Pak would ask them to do my chores and they had no choice but to obey her orders.

Only ten months or so into my schooling, my kindergarten teacher committed suicide. Of course, I didn't quite know that at the time, only that there was much activity one morning as we were herded into our class one minute and sent home the next. I had liked the teacher very much. She never once made me feel like I didn't belong, or wasn't as smart as the other children, or didn't deserve the same attention and care as everyone else. The classroom was magical, and I suspect it set me up for loving education ever since.

Classes were suspended for over a week, as there were no other teachers or schools near the temple. I was so devastated to learn about the death of my teacher that I did not speak for this entire period. I kept silent, performed my chores dutifully, and did everything Ah Pak asked of me without complaining. If magic was to die, I would not celebrate life.

But we were sent back to school two weeks later. And with the resilience of children—a kind of magic in itself—I started to speak and play again.

My vocabulary expanded quickly, and I was able to read in complete sentences, then complete paragraphs and, finally, whole stories. From time to time, worshippers would bring us treats wrapped in newspapers, and I would read the stories, ads, and comic strips. This was how I learned to read French. Even though English is the official language, French has been widely used since Mauritius was established, spoken all over the island in commerce, homes, and the workplace. However, 90 percent of the population speaks Mauritian Creole, or Morisien, which serves as the de facto native language and mother tongue.

One day, while the girls and I were speaking half Creole and half Hakka (our way of sharing secrets if we didn't want Ah Pak to know what we were plotting), Mr. Chui walked into the pagoda. He told me much later that he had been surprised to hear me mix French in with my Creole. He asked if I would like to attend a real school and how would I feel about being away from the pagoda during school days. I do not recall the rest. All I remember is that shortly after, I was enrolled in a primary school.

The academic year in Mauritius starts in January and ends in early November with a four-week break in July. The year I turned six, I was told that I would be attending Villiers René Government School because Park, Mr. Chui's son, was already there and I could walk with him to school. It was proposed that I would live with the Chui family from Monday to Thursday. Mr. and Mrs. Chui had five sons and nine daughters, making for a very busy and very crowded household. And yet, there always seemed to be room for me.

Ah Yan, one of Mr. Chui's employees, was tasked with driving me back to the pagoda on Friday after school. On Sunday afternoons, he would pick me up again to join the Chui family for dinner and return to school from there the next morning. This arrangement was agreed upon between Ah Pak and Mr. Chui. Ah Pak managed to secure another concession: that I could be called upon to skip school at any point to help with the chores at the pagoda.

Shu walked me to school on the morning of the first day. It was only a couple of houses down from Mr. Chui's residence—I had passed it many times before but never really noticed it. I marvelled to see so many boys and girls running around, dozens and dozens, playing tag, hide and seek, jumping rope, and marbles. I had not seen so many boys and girls in one place before and, for a moment, was unsure if I was dreaming. Then Shu pulled my hand, and we continued walking. As we passed a group of boys playing marbles, I was transfixed by the mosaic of colours in the little glass balls. I stopped, wanting to touch them, but Shu kept pulling my hand to keep walking. She scolded me, saying that only boys play with marbles. Girls can skip rope and play hide-and-seek, she said. None of this made sense to me, and still doesn't.

Shu registered me under my birth name Oi-Chu Shiu. She introduced herself to the principal as my guardian and the older sister of Park. She assured the principal that I was a well-behaved student, not like her brother, and that they should not have any problems with me.

The school was housed in an imposing three-storey building. Each storey had four classrooms, with a big courtyard between the principal's office and the building. The principal walked us to my classroom and told me this was Standard I (grade one), Section C, with Mr. Raoul.

Once at the classroom door, we were greeted by Mr. Raoul, a young, soft-spoken and well-mannered teacher. Shu told him that I was anxious, and he assured me that all the pupils were anxious, as it was our first day of real school and we were away from our families. There must have been at least twenty children in my class. The majority were of East Indian descent, plus a handful of Asian and Black pupils. The girls wore colourful dresses and had long braided hair, a stark contrast to my plain dress and plain ponytail. I wore mostly the same dresses to school; my whole wardrobe could fit into a backpack. Shu graciously had a dress made to measure for me every Chinese New Year.

I loved school and learning. But staying with the Chui family during the week was proving surprisingly difficult. Though they fed me well and cared for me, and I did not have to do any chores other than to study or complete my homework, I was never at home or at ease living there. I felt like an intruder and even a second-class citizen. The class difference was impossible to ignore. Back at the pagoda, we were all equal and I could relax. No one was judging me or feeling sorry for me. At the Chui's, however, though I had no idea if they were judging or pitying me, I was nonetheless reminded of everything I did not have. I did not have material goods or a grand house. But most of all, I did not have a family. Every Friday I waited impatiently for the driver to pick me up and take me back to the pagoda.

Ah Yan was one of Mr. Chui's most trusted employees. In the beginning, the trip from the Chui residence to the pagoda seemed long, as both Ah Yan and I would be silent in our thoughts. But gradually, he started asking me about school and what I had learned. His voice was soft and friendly and made me want to talk to him. He told me he liked driving me around even though it cut his weekend short. He shared stories with me of his adventures driving around the island and delivering tea for Mr. Chui.

Once, mid-week, Ah Yan had to take me back to the pagoda because Ah Pak needed me to help with something—probably the preparation of a deity's birthday ceremony or a service for a deceased Chinese Buddhist. The nuns performed the last rites, which included a long service with chants, followed by tea. As well, after the burial or cremation, the nuns would be asked to perform religious memorial services in the pagoda where all the family members would be invited to participate in the chants. The memorial services could last for one or two days. Since there were only five of us and everyone would be busy, they needed me to stay with Koung Koung to keep her company.

Once, when I was not much older than ten, Lan was ill, and I had to take her place to perform the last rites. I was asked to chant along with the nuns at an altar in front of the open casket. It was my first time doing that, and later that night I could not sleep and had nightmares for days.

I secretly prayed that nobody would die on a school day, as Ah Yan, busy with more important tasks, would not be able to take me back to the pagoda. He would often ask me if I had any idea as to how long I would be away from school and if I liked missing school. My usual answer would be, "I don't know but Shu, Mr. Chui's older daughter, will let you know when to come pick me up."

I had mixed feelings about missing school. While I was happy to be back at the pagoda with Lan and

Fen, I hated missing school because I had to catch up on everything I had missed. Back then, it was not the teacher's responsibility to re-teach what you had missed. I must have missed at least a couple hundred school days throughout the primary grades. Each time, I would return to school with a note from Shu stating illness as the reason for my absence, which was of course not true.

My first year at Villiers René was fun and went by quickly. I learned to read and write in English and French, and I excelled in arithmetic. I would finish my classwork early most of the time and Mr. Raoul would show me how to add and subtract two- and three-digit numbers with and without regrouping. He would let me flip through the dictionary and learn new words.

I paid attention to Mr. Raoul's lessons and followed his classroom rules. I was obedient, courteous, and quiet. Nonetheless, I had trouble making friends because I did not know how to play games or make conversation. Mostly, however, I kept my distance because I did not want my classmates to know that I was an orphan. My classmates went home to their families every day after school, while I did not. How could they understand my situation?

The school day was sandwiched between a lunch hour and two small breaks, one in the morning and one in the afternoon. I spent recesses walking around in the courtyard alone or helping Mr. Raoul with chores, such as sharpening the pencils or collecting the notebooks from pupils' desks. He always called on me to do these things, a kindness and generosity that took me a few years to appreciate.

At lunchtime, Park would stay at school playing ball or marbles with his classmates while I walked back to the Chui's house. He would pretend that he did not know me when I asked to play. Instead, he rebuked me and sent me away. I quickly learned to stay away from him and joined him in this pretense that we did not know each other. We only spoke when he needed my help with schoolwork.

At the end of each year, I obtained the highest marks in all the subjects and was awarded prizes. The prizes, dictionaries or pen and pencil sets were awarded at a ceremony where parents and family members were invited. But I never let Shu or Ah Pak know about the awards. I especially did not let Ah Pak worry that I was doing too well at school. If she thought she might lose an extra pair of hands to do the chores, she might pull me out of class entirely.

Once, however, she found one of my prizes, a new Parker fountain pen. She asked if she could use it to write her chants. I gifted it to her, with thanks for letting me go to school. She put up a front as if she was angry at me for spending so much time on my studies instead of reading the scriptures or chants. However, I suspected she was proud of my achievement and successes. I witnessed exchanges between her and the Chui family, where the latter would complain about Park's poor performance. I could tell she was silently proud.

I lived with the Chui family until I turned eight. When I was in Standard IV (grade four), it was decided that I would once again return to the pagoda full-time, as I was older and ready to share the workload with Lan and Fen. It was made clear that chores at the pagoda had priority over study time and schoolwork. I would go to school only when there were no ceremonies or services, which once again made my attendance inconsistent and unpredictable. Also, Ah Yan could no longer drive me.

Ah Pak found another driver to take me to school, and I joined a car-pooling service. Since I lived the furthest from the city, Ah Vee Ko picked me up first at 7:30 a.m. in his Volkswagen Beetle for the monthly fee of forty rupees. Next, he collected another girl and two other boys, dropping the girl off at Loreto Convent School and finally, the two boys and me to Villiers René. We arrived at school between 8:30 and 8:45 a.m., depending on how punctual the girl was, and she mostly wasn't. We sometimes had to wait long minutes for her, always worried that she would make us late for school.

I usually either read or studied for tests as we drove. I liked studying or daydreaming in the car because the other children were half asleep and it was calm. I enjoyed my quiet and peaceful ride—until I was a little bit older. By then it felt tedious, and I wondered aloud if the boys and I could be dropped off first instead of last. I specifically told Ah Vee Ko that it wasn't fair that I was the first to be picked up and the last to be dropped off, especially as our collective punctuality depended so often on the girl.

When my request fell on deaf ears, one morning I asked Ah Vee Ko what would happen if we got to

50

school late, and who would be responsible for speaking with the principal about our tardiness. I wondered, in order to avoid this problem, if he could pick us up even earlier because I was up at 5 a.m. every morning anyway. He reassured me that we would not be late getting to school. Running out of ideas, I suggested that perhaps he could pick up the girl last to give her more time to get ready. He told me that no matter how much time we gave the girl, she would always be late and that he had mapped out the most direct routes to get all of us to school. He turned his head to the back of the car and asked, "Why do you have to get to school so early? Are you conducting some business there? Stay away from trouble or Ah Pak will take you out of school!"

From that conversation, I learned not to push my luck and to put up with the situation. I also eventually realized that Ah Vee Ko did not feel comfortable pushing the girl's parents to get her ready faster because they were wealthy, and she was the only child. No matter what was happening on the clock, we were on that girl's time, and not ours.

I put up with her tardiness until the end of elementary school. It was a lesson in how life is unfair, how money speaks, and that if I wanted to be listened to, I needed to be able to command respect. As I had no wealth, my only hope in that regard was my intelligence. To make a bad situation better, I used my car ride time to think of essay topics I could write about or expand my general knowledge and study for my tests or exams. Money was power but so, I was beginning to hope, was knowledge.

There were four sections in each Standard: Section A was for the top students, Section B was for the above average students, Section C was for the average to below average students, and Section D was for students who had learning difficulties or who had to repeat a grade. I wanted to be in Section A throughout my schooling at Villiers René. This would give me status and prestige, I thought, and make me feel like I was somebody. From then on, I was always in Section A. As well, I skipped two grades, and by Standard VI, I had caught up with Park. We were not in the same class, as he was in D and I was in A. This was a small consolation.

By the time I graduated, after seven years of schooling, I was among the top five percent scorers for the Certificate of Primary Education and was accepted to one of the most prestigious all-girl schools: Loreto Convent School.

Loreto Convent was very big, with vast open spaces and playgrounds, several volleyball pitches, a basketball court and, more recently, a tennis court. Inside, the gymnasium had space for every sport and activity, including table tennis. Today, there is even an audio-visual room with computers and smart boards. The school was incredibly active, with an annual school mass, a prize-giving ceremony, a music day and an annual sports day. As a non-Catholic, I looked forward to participating in the mass as it gave me a chance to read the Bible, learn about Jesus Christ, and participate in the singing.

I loved that Loreto Convent students wore the same uniform, regardless of our class, race, colour, or religion.

But it was a one-size-fits-all educational system, where we were prepared for the A-level examinations administered by Cambridge University. Although the institution followed the government curriculum, they were ahead of their time and taught issues such as social justice, civil rights, women's rights, and so on. We were encouraged to discuss, debate and voice our opinions and views on topics and issues that were of interest to us.

One room I vividly remember is the very large kitchen where we took Home Economics. Between classes I would linger outside just to smell the delicious baked cookies and breads. I vividly remember the time we had to make a pound cake for an assignment. Unfortunately, my cake came out of the oven looking like someone had flattened it with an iron. It elicited lots of laughter and jokes among classmates, but my teacher was not in the mood for that and reprimanded both me and the students. I was disappointed with myself. I don't know what came over me, but I took the pound cake to my desk, sat down, and in one bite ate the whole thing before the teacher had a chance to taste it and give me a grade. She gave me detention for my misbehaviour and marked me 9/20 for the assignment.

The Home Economics teacher was Samantha Chui— as it turned out, Mr. Chui's daughter-in-law. After my detention, I went to the tea store where I told Mr. Chui what had happened. He listened, attentive to what I could only see as my grand misfortune. Several times, I broke down in tears recounting what I had done. I did not understand the smile that he was desperately trying to hide.

53

"It's only one course," he said. "You don't have to take Home Economics for your O level and you cannot be good at everything."

"But I have to be good at everything," I said, "or else I will not make it for the Cambridge O Level and escape my life at the pagoda. Don't you understand this?" He could not possibly understand how, for me, everything mattered, and one wrong move could send me hurtling back to nothingness.

"What do you want me to do?"

"I want you to speak with Samantha and ask her to give me an extra point so I can pass my Home Economics class. Could you please speak to her? Please?" I could have said *please* a hundred times more but stopped myself. Mr. Chui would not appreciate the begging, no matter how compassionate he may have been.

"I will think about it. But life has challenges, and you must find solutions to overcome them. This is one such challenge. Can you study harder for your class? Perhaps your teacher can give you an extra assignment to make up for the bad cake? His eyes twinkled. "Or can you ask for Samantha's help yourself ?"

That seemed like an impossible task. "No. I don't want to ask her for help. She is strict and not approachable."

Mr. Chui stood up and signalled that the conversation had ended. Perhaps I had insulted his daughter-in-law, or perhaps I had gone too far in my pleading for perfection. Probably both. I wished I could fly away and disappear. I did not revisit this incident or the Home Economics class with him again, and he did not ask.

But I made every effort to work even harder. At the end of the year, I was given a passing grade for the course. I could have fainted with relief.

Overall, secondary schooling was a challenge. I did not receive a single prize at Loreto Convent. I was an average student in every sense of the word. I was not rich, did not have high grades, was just okay in sports, and did not participate in extracurricular activities—indeed, I was not allowed, as I had to work at the pagoda every day after school. I did make a few good friends and I had one best friend, Isabelle. She and I would do our homework and study together. She was outgoing, kind and pleasant to be around. We did not see each other on the weekend, as she lived quite far away. She took the bus to come to school and at the end of the day needed to catch it almost immediately to return home.

I eventually lost contact with all my friends. They all got married after high school and none of them pursued a post-secondary education. No one could have predicted that, despite being raised as an orphan, I would be the one to go on to university. It was thanks to the support of Mr. Chui. I hold him in the highest esteem, and he deserves all the credit for the person that I was to become.

Chapter 6

THE CHUI FAMILY

I was in Mr. Raj's class and Park Chui was in Madame Poutou's Standard VI (grade six). Park was a slim, handsome, chatty boy, his mother's favourite. His nickname in Hakka was Kai Kai Cou, meaning chatterbox. Park had some behavioural and learning problems at school and compensated by becoming the class clown. He was inattentive and disruptive, and often got detention or would be made to write lines as punishment, such as "I will not be disruptive in class while lessons are in progress." Because Mrs. Chui did not speak Creole, she would send her older daughter, Shu, to speak to Park's teachers.

I often helped Park complete his homework while he was copying lines. Helping him with his homework gave me something to do after dinner. In the beginning, I was only able to solve his basic math problems. But as my vocabulary and command of Creole, French and English increased, I was able to help Park with the rest of his schoolwork, which consisted of conjugating verbs, using vocabulary in a sentence, or filling in the blanks. By Standard IV, I was doing all his language exercises while he played with the dogs in the courtyard.

One day, Park came home walking funny. He said he had been beaten by his teacher for not completing his work and for being inattentive in class. I was angry beyond words; I suggested that he ask his father to speak with the principal and that his teacher be fired for beating him up. He told me that it was not such a good idea because if his father knew, he would be grounded for months. I told him to consider wearing extra thick underwear and a second pair of pants. He thought this was a great idea.

The next time the teacher beat him, Park let me know that my suggestion had worked. Even so, he had screamed just as loudly so as not to raise suspicions. I told him that he was getting smarter and that perhaps he could consider being less talkative and disruptive if he wanted the punishments to stop altogether. He just laughed. He left school a couple of years later to work with his brother, Hu, in their father's store.

There were usually a couple of maids taking care of us. I chatted with them as they did their chores. I learned how to wash dishes properly, how to iron dresses and blouses, and how to cut vegetables. They cooked their own meals, which consisted of rice and bread with curried vegetables and anchovies stewed with tomatoes and green chillies. The whole kitchen would smell of anchovies and I did my best not to be around then, as I did not want my hair to have a fishy smell. I refused to eat the stinky anchovies, and in fact my first taste of anchovies would not be until I had them on a pizza in Canada. In turn, the maids did not want to taste any Asian food. The only concession they made was for the delicious Chinese noodles with tomato and coriander chutney that Mrs. Chui made.

Most of the helpers came from small villages or hamlets, where boys would work in the sugar cane fields or tea plantations and girls found employment in the cities as maids. Often, scouting couples or families would pluck young girls and take them home with them. Once, Shu brought back a young maid of fifteen from Rivière du Rempart, a small village in the northeast of the island. The maid, Susie, cried at night and begged every day to go home to her family. I spent many nights with her until we were both tired and she stopped crying. She ended up staying with the Chui family for the full year before returning to her hometown. She taught me some new Creole words and I learned all about her family, including her brothers and sisters. Generally, the maids liked me because I never acted as if they were beneath me. Plus, it was through interacting with them that I discovered words or expressions that I did not learn at school.

On rare occasions, Park's mother would be home and she would make us her favourite dish: beef and cauliflower with rice. I hated it but ate it to fill my stomach and be polite. She sat at the dining table and watched us eat. Despite being told politely and repeatedly that my digestive system did not tolerate meat, she insisted on putting it on my plate. When she was not watching, I would feed the slices of beef to the dogs. It wasn't long before the dogs were always following me, tails wagging. When it came time to return to school after lunch, I had to trick them by throwing a ball far from the door that led to rue La Paix so they would not follow me.

Sometimes I would give the meat to Park, and he would put it in the pockets of his shorts where he'd feed it later to the dogs or, more likely, forget about it. The maids complained to his mother, who was angry at him for wrecking his shorts. One day I had the idea to put the uneaten meat in a plastic bag. I left it in my pocket for the whole day and, just before going to the shower, gave the meat to the dogs. The plastic bag had acted as a barrier and protected the pocket of my clothes. I shared my discovery with Park and suggested that he always keep a small plastic bag in his pocket, just in case. He did so, but then did not take the time to put his food properly in the plastic bag. The food would still come in direct contact with his pocket and would ruin his clothes.

Hu was a year older than Park. He was sporty and had many friends with whom he hung around. He was nice in his younger years, even sometimes asking me what I was working on or what I had learned at school. He was only home at mealtimes because he was in Form II at Bhujoharry College with his sister Heather, who was in Form V, preparing for her school certificate. Heather had a sarcastic demeanour. When she was not busy studying or finishing her homework, she would chat and tease me. For example, she would laugh at the way I spoke Creole, supposedly with a Hakka accent.

I was not close to Heather, nor with Hu or Louise. I tried to have very little to do with them, even when I was under their roof. All three of them had an air of superiority which I did not like.

Once Hu finished his Cambridge school certificate, he was asked by his parents to help out in the Bois Chéri tea store. We saw each other more during this period, but his demeanour had changed. Now he was intent on maintaining an air of authority, and so we fought like cats and dogs. He called me names and I talked back to him. I even punched him a few times in front of Mr. and Mrs. Chui. They asked Hu to stop teasing me and calling me names, and they did not discipline me for punching their son.

Louise, the second youngest of the family, spent much of her time sitting at her desk doing homework or studying for her exams. She attended London College and was in Form IV. With her shoulder-length black hair and dark glasses, she had a studious and serious air. We did not like each other, despite having to share a bed. She often complained about my moving too much at night or hogging her side of the bed. Mr. Chui would ask her to be more tolerant and to make life easier for all parties concerned. Heather and Louise would often argue, and I would stay in the courtyard with the maids and the dogs until it was time for me to go to bed.

To avoid them as much as possible, I went to bed after they did, sneaking under the mosquito net onto the bed I shared with Louise. More often than not I would get entangled in the netting and had to undo my limbs without disturbing the person next to me.

Chapter 7

BOIS CHÉRI

Mr. Chui was the sole distributor of Bois Chéri, a popular Mauritian tea company. Years later, when "Mr. Bois Chéri," as he was sometimes referred to, retired and passed on his company to his successors, the Bois Chéri company unfortunately took the opportunity to do business with another distributor. And so, after a few decades in business, Mr. Chui's tea store closed its doors.

I have many fond memories of the tea store. Upon entering, one could smell the vanilla and tea leaves. There was a desk on the right where Shu and Heng, Shu's husband, took clients' orders. In the middle of the store was Mr. Chui's executive desk and a grey leather chair. He was both manager and cashier. He worked from 7 a.m. to 5 p.m., Monday to Friday. On Saturdays, he worked until 1 p.m., when the store closed. He was the only person who handled cash when Hu and Park were in school. He did not trust his money with anyone and certainly not with his gambling wife.

I started going to the store after school with Park when we were in Standard VI. Mr. Chui would ask

63

if we were hungry or if we wanted to have a snack, sometimes giving us 2 rupees to get something from Mr. Fred's convenience store, a few metres away. I would buy pickled cucumber and candies and bring them back to the store to share with everyone. Mr. Chui would grimace with disapproval and say, "You need to eat real food. This is not good for you. You will get a stomach ache or diarrhea."

I held up a pickle. "Try one, you'll like it too."

He just grimaced even more. One day I caught him in a good mood. He finally took a bite of my pickle, but hated it so much he jumped to the sidewalk and spit it out on the street.

I laughed so loud that Park said, "Ena bez ar twa," meaning, *You are something*.

Mr. Chui commanded respect and nobody dared to fool around with him, but I did and from that day on, there was a subtle change in the air. Perhaps because I had gone unpunished, people began to respect and listen to me. When I asked his employees to use the boxes of tea to make me a table so I could do my home-work, they did so without insisting I get permission first from Mr. Chui. In fact, when he saw it, Mr. Chui made sure the table was the right height and comfortable. He said if it wasn't I should ask one of the employees to adjust the boxes for me. There was not a high turnover of employees, even though Mr. Chui was strict with them. Underneath his stern facade, he was a compas-sionate and kind man and his employees liked working with him. They were from all backgrounds and races: some were Muslim, some were Indian, some were

African, and others were Asian. He treated them all with dignity, fairness and respect. He cared for their well-being and fed or gave them extra money when they faced challenges or hardship.

Long after I graduated from primary school and left their residence, I returned to the store almost daily. I would walk from the Loreto Convent College to rue Léoville L'Homme and would spend a couple of hours chatting with Park, Shu and Mrs. Chui. When I missed my ride from Ah Vee Ko after school, Mr. Chui would ask Heng or Ah Yan, and later Park when he got his driver's license, to drive me back to the pagoda. Often, he would insist that I have dinner with his family first. He wanted to make sure I was well nourished, he would say.

I did not like getting rides to go back to the pagoda. When I was in Form IV at the Loreto Convent, Park put me at the back of the Peugeot van with three cages of livestock. The chickens were flapping their wings next to me, and I screamed all the way home. The next day, I told Mr. Chui that I no longer wanted to get a ride from Park as I had been forced to share the backseat with the livestock. I saw the faint smile on Mr. Chui's face. "Then how are you going to get back to the pagoda?" and I responded by saying I did not know. Mr. Chui asked what the agreed time for Ah Vee Ko was to pick me up from school and whether arrangements could be made for Ah Vee Ko to pick me up from his store.

Ah Vee Ko had prescribed schedules of pick-up and drop-off. He had at least twelve students whom he took to various schools on any given day. So, it was either

I took my ride from Ah Vee Ko to go to the pagoda after school or put up with Park's way of getting me to bond with the livestock. I liked being with Park so in the end I decided to miss my ride back to the pagoda and put up with chickens.

To this day, I believe that was the one of best decisions I ever made. By observing Mr. Chiu and his family interact with different retailers and peddlers from across the island, I gained valuable knowledge. I even made acquaintances with a few of them, and they would strike up a conversation or two, asking how old I was and whether I was still at school, what the names of my parents were and if it was my mother or father who was the daughter or son of Mr. Chui. In return, I would ask, "Where is your store? What do you sell there? How much are you going to sell the tea for?" Some would share their plans or prices; others would find me too nosy for asking so many questions. Mr. Chui would sit in his leather chair, listening to our conversations, smiling and looking at the street as if he was waiting for some merchants to enter his store. Our eyes would meet sometimes, and I quickly learned it was his way of telling me to shut up.

Mr. Chui had a verbal contract agreement with the retailers in which the latter would pay only once they sold the tea, usually towards the end of the month. If the retailers did not pay at the end of the month, they would not be able to get any more merchandise until they had paid their debts. Stores are closed on Thursday afternoon in the Plaines Wilhems district, so retailers go to Port Louis to replenish their stocks and pay their debts. Thursday afternoon was usually a busy time at the store with retailers occupied with buying and paying their debts. Mr. Chui appreciated the extra help when I showed up after school. Most of the time, there was only Shu and him taking care of the retailers from Plaines Wilhems, while Park, Hu and Heng were out taking orders from surrounding retailers. When I got older, he would ask me to help him with the orders of the merchants or check if we had enough stock to sell to the retailers. I liked helping him. I would list all the items on the order form for the merchants and pass the lists to him to affix the prices, as there were so many varieties of tea and I had not remembered the prices yet.

I was always intrigued as to the reasons Mr. Chui would not label the price of each item in his store. At closing time on a busy Thursday, I decided to ask Mr. Chui if he would like me to help him label the price of the different teas so I could complete the purchasing transactions without having him to complete my orders. He did not say a word or acknowledge my request. It fell on deaf ears, or so it seemed.

That afternoon, I got a bit annoyed and wondered if I had done something wrong or said something that Mr. Chui did not approve of. I could not come up with an answer. So, on my ride to the pagoda, I told Park about how my offer to help had remained unacknowledged. I further stated that if there were a price on the items, I could easily complete the orders. He told me that it was more complicated than it looked. I needed to know all the retailers, their relationship with the store, their credit rating, their trustworthiness and so on. That was why his father liked to handle the last segment of the transaction. I said, "Oh! I thought Mr. Chui was mad at me for something."

Park laughed and, just before we got to the pagoda, said, "Dad likes you a great deal. In his eyes, you are the smartest of all."

"OK, then," was all I could manage. "See you tomorrow."

That night, I thought of what Park had said. I revisited several times my interactions with the retailers, Mr. Chui and Shu. I still could not understand why Mr. Chui would not respond to my request to let me affix the price on each item. But I also reminded myself that I wanted to feel welcome when I was at the store and so I should not make any fuss. After all, it was his store and he could do whatever he wanted.

A few weeks passed and one Thursday afternoon, when I got to the store there was a retailer in a seeming state of distress, sitting in front of Mr. Chui. I walked in quietly, said hello, and proceeded to put my school bag on top of a box of tea. No one seemed to notice that I was in the store and so I sat down next to Shu and started a conversation with her. She asked me about how my day at school had gone and I asked her what was going on between the retailer, Mr. Jean, and Mr. Chui. I later learned that the former had not paid his debt for the last three months. I did not see any anger from Mr. Chui or violent exchanges between them. But I sensed the gravity of the conversation. I could not report what was the decision reached, as Park had to be somewhere early that evening and wanted to drop me off at the pagoda on his way.

There was another incident that reinforced my respect for Mr. Chui. Mr. Li, who came from China, was unemployed and raising a young family of three. He asked Mr. Chui to help him find a job. Mr. Li was married to Hannah, who was my nanny and whom I called Mom. Hannah had been Ah Pak's best friend and confidante. When Ah Pak brought me to Mauritius, she asked Hannah if she could take care of me given that Ah Pak never had children of her own and did not know how to raise an infant. Since Hannah's children, Steve, Seth, and Francine, were much older and did not need their mother to care for them as much, Hannah accepted to be my nanny. Steve, Seth, and Francine became my adopted siblings. Hannah was a wonderful, caring and loving mother. She taught me love, compassion, and loyalty. She treated me as one of her own children. I did not know her husband Mr. Li as well; when he was not working, he was spending time playing cards in a Chinese Club with his friends.

Mr. Chui found Mr. Li a job as a delivery man for a cigarette manufacturer, Mills Company. Mr. Li worked for Mills for several years before he was let go due to narcolepsy, a chronic sleep disorder. Mills Company informed Mr. Chui of Mr. Li's dismissal. Shortly after his dismissal, Mr. Li came to buy a pack of tea for his family at the tea store and told Mr. Chui that he had not stolen anything from Mills, as they had accused him but could not prove this, but that he often found it difficult to stay awake for long periods of time. Instead

69

of keeping an eye on the driver, he was sleeping and could not account for the missing boxes of cigarettes. Every afternoon Mills would detain Mr. Li to interrogate him until he was let go. He shared this information with Mr. Chui. The latter continued to treat him kindly and respectfully and even gave him a discount and an extra pack of tea. In fact, Mr. Li would drop by the store to chat with Mr. Chui from time to time.

Mr. Chui was a man of great foresight, thoughtful, kind, generous, and non-judgmental. He had many friends, although I can't remember the names of any of them. I remember that he and his friends would walk two to three laps of a horse racetrack, called Champs de Mars, every morning at 5 a.m. His friends would come and buy tea from him, and he would always give them a big discount.

When I was in Form V (grade 11), Mr. Chui bought three brand new Honda mopeds, two blue ones and a red one, for his employees to run small errands around the city. I ended up having a blue one with the licence plate BS 169, even though I did not know how to ride a bicycle. He asked me to take one of the mopeds so that I did not have to rely on anyone to take me to school or bring me back to the pagoda. He paid for everything, and I practiced driving the moped in the alley, against the hedges in case I fell. I did crash once, and the hedges helped, though I did burn my leg badly against the hot chain guard. However, two weeks later, I was ready to ride the moped to school. I decided that I would wake up at 4 a.m. to do all my chores and leave the pagoda at 6:45 a.m., when there was little traffic, and get to the tea store at 7 a.m. I would leave my moped at the store and walk to Loreto convent, because of the busy traffic in the morning before and after school. In the afternoon, I would walk back to the store and, when the store closed, I would ride my moped back to the pagoda. The moped gave me the freedom to leave the store when I wanted.

I would be the first one waiting for Mr. Chui to open the store. He would ask me to go upstairs to have breakfast with Park, Hu and Mrs. Chui. Sometimes, I would have breakfast with them. But I usually pre-ferred to stay with him in the store, as it was quiet, calm and the smell of tea relaxed me and prepared me for the day.

Mr. Chui was more of a listener than a talker. He was a master teacher. There are few master teachers in life, as most of us are still learning. But Mr. Chui could listen to life so well that he could hear the vastness in everything and in me. He had found a way to listen well. Most of the time, we would sit looking outside the display windows without saying a word to one another. There were times when I would ask him how his walk was or when the big truck from Bois Chéri would be coming to replenish the stock. Many years later, I real-ized that I may have learned the secret of listening from Mr. Chui, but I will never learn the secrets of life because I will have to listen for myself.

He usually had his breakfast at 7:30 a.m., and so I would be holding the fort while he went upstairs to eat. He would let me be both the cashier and manager while he was temporarily away. I loved being given

71

the responsibility, as it showed that I was trusted and responsible.

By then, most of the employees were at the store and I would ensure that they were at their posts performing their duties. I remember a few of the younger employees did not take me seriously. They would defy my requests and would let me know in no uncertain terms that I was not their boss and they did not have to listen to me. I would calmly tell them that I was in charge and that I would let Mr. Chui, who was also referred to as Bonhomme, know of their disrespect.

As soon as he finished breakfast, he would come down to the store and before he could even have a chance to sit on his chair, I had already told him what so-and-so had said and done during his absence. I would ask him to remind the employees that I was in charge when he was not there. To my big surprise, he advocated for me. He told his employees to take my requests seriously and that there was no room for disrespectful or inappropriate behaviour in the store. He called on them for mutual respect and a peaceful working environment. What I heard made me respect him and hold him in high regard. I worked hard to show him that I was trustworthy, capable, fair and just.

There was a homeless Asian man who lived on the street where the store was located. He would not take any food from anyone. He had a great deal of pride and rumour had it that he came from a rich family and that, when he had lost his wife, he had fallen into depression and ended up on the street. I would see him lying on the pavement at the corner of the store every day; on multiple occasions I offered him the pickles or the soda or candies I bought from Mr. Fred's convenience store, but he would look away. He would poke his head inside the store around 8 a.m. every morning, Monday to Saturday, and he would accept the one rupee Mr. Chui offered him. He would bow his head and smile because he was deaf, or so I was told.

On several occasions, Mr. Chui was with clients when the homeless man dropped by, and so I asked Mr. Chui for one rupee to give him. I would hand him the rupee, but he would not take it from me. He would look away and stand at the door until Mr. Chui stopped what he was doing and gave him the money. He would buy food to feed himself for the day. I was both puzzled and miffed. I shared this incident with Park, Hu, Shu and Heng and even Ah Yan. They all told me that the man was strange and to leave him alone. I decided to ask Mr. Chui why this man would not even take one rupee from me.

Mr. Chui smiled and said: "Beggars are human beings, like you and me. We don't know what happened to them in their past life. Nobody wants to be a beggar or homeless. But circumstances put them in the position they are in, and we need to show them we care and respect them. Try showing him you care and maybe he will accept your offerings."

Mr. Chui's message was loud and clear. We all want to preserve our dignity and be respected, regardless of who we are or what we have become. I continued to offer him the snacks I had bought from Mr. Fred's convenience store when I passed him until, one day out of nowhere, he reached out his hand. I knelt and gave him a Kit Kat bar. He looked me in the eyes and gave me a smile. I thanked him for allowing me to share my snacks with him, then off to the store I went.

Excited, I shared my interaction with the homeless man with Mr. Chui and the latter smiled and said, "You need to be patient and you need to let people know you are sincere and can be trusted."

From that day onward, when the homeless man showed up at the store at 8 a.m., Mr. Chui gave me a rupee from the cash register to give to him. I put the rupee in the palm of his hand. He looked at us both, bowed and left.

The Chui family and the employees could not believe their eyes when they saw that the homeless man would take things from me when they had previously tried unsuccessfully to offer him food or drinks of various kinds. The following year, as food prices were going up, Mr. Chui decided to give him two rupees. Every morning for the next few years, I gave him two rupees before I left for school.

As the years passed, the homeless man's clothes got dirtier, shabbier and smellier. I asked Mr. Chui for his thoughts about giving some of his old shirts to the man. Mr. Chui responded, "I think you are asking a lot from the man."

"Did you see how dirty and how torn out his clothes are," I asked Mr. Chui. "He smells and he badly needs a shower. Does he have a name?"

"He likes it that way. Let him be thus, so long as he is fed and healthy."

"Where is his family? Does he have one?" I thought for a minute. "Or maybe he doesn't have a family, like me?"

Mr. Chui frowned. "Stop! We are your family. We will look after you, care for you and love you, OK?"

I was both taken aback and touched. The conversation ended and we never discussed the homeless man's hygiene again.

One day much later, on my way to the store, I saw the homeless man wearing Mr. Chui's blue shirt, one of the shirts that Mr. Chui bought by the half dozen at a time.

"When did you give him the shirt? Did you know he was going to wear it?"

"It doesn't matter when I gave it to him. He is wearing it and I am happy, and I know you are, too."

"Yeah, I am, and he looks better. Maybe you should give him your sandals."

"You want him to have new clothes, and now you want him to have sandals too! Come on. Relax a bit."

"He has bare feet. And maybe you can get him to take a shower!"

Park, who was nearby, spoke up. "I hope you are not asking for the man to come into our house to have a shower!"

"Yes, why not," I answered sincerely. "He is a human being."

Park just laughed out loud while Mr. Chui observed our interactions with each other.

From then on, every time I passed the homeless man on the street, he would bow whether or not I had snacks for him. I am glad he had allowed me to get to know him a little bit.

Before I left Mauritius for my studies in Toronto, I spoke with the homeless man one last time. I told him that he would not be seeing me around for a while, as I was leaving to further my education abroad. I assured him that Mr. Chui would always be there if he needed something. He gave me a big smile, a smile I would never forget.

A couple of years later when I came back to visit the island, the first thing I noticed was that the homeless man was not on the pavement at the corner of the store. I asked Park and Mr. Chui about him and learned that he had passed away. Park told me that his father had arranged for the homeless man's burial and that he was now resting in peace.

Many years have passed since Mr. Chui's generosity, compassion, and love carried me through challenging times. He taught me kindness, compassion, and love. He represents the humanity that is found in mankind.

When my sons and I were in Mauritius in February 2013, I learned from Park that his mother had also passed on. He took us to the cemetery to pay our respects to his parents. As I stood at the foot of their tombs, tears ran down my cheeks. I thanked them for their love, kindness, and care. I introduced them to my two boys and again thanked Mr. Chui for advocating for me to have an education to become the best educator I could be. Park held my arm and said, "I know dad loved and cared so much for you. He is happy for your successes, I am sure. You will be OK."

My interactions with the Chui family, their employees, the merchants, and the tea store were part of my childhood. They have all contributed and shaped the person I am today. The store closed its doors for good in 2013, a few days after my visit with the boys. I asked Hu, who has made the second floor of the store his permanent residence, if the boys and I could have dinner with him. I wanted to recreate and share the happy memories of my childhood hanging around in the store. It was a dinner not like any other. I told stories to my boys and Hu of growing up in this place. I laughed and cried. The pictures of Mr. and Mrs. Chui on the wall by the dining table further reminded us of them, of the meals I shared with them, and of our conversations. I miss them dearly.

Park and Shu told us details of their father's funeral. Mr. Chui had a traditional funeral with an open casket. The visitations took place on the second floor of the tea store. Mr. Chui's family walked behind his coffin in a procession on rue Léoville L'Homme. Many dignitaries, local merchants, friends and family, and present and past employees joined his family in the procession.

One of Mrs. Chui's daughters told me that Mr. Chui had been very sick but was quite lucid in the end. His children and grandchildren all gathered around his bedside when the doctors told the family that he would not make it for another day. Despite that he kept repeating, "I still have to wait for one more child." He waited two more days before drawing his last breath. He was waiting for me to say goodbye until we would meet again someday.

I was unable to make it to Mr. Chui's funeral. In Mauritius, when someone dies and is not embalmed, the funeral needs to take place within 24 hours. Given that it takes over 20 hours by air to get to Mauritius from Toronto, and in the late 80s there were no daily flights from London to Mauritius, this was problematic to say the least. Furthermore, the airfare to Mauritius was substantial and I had just started a new teaching job. Do I regret not attending Mr. Chui's funeral? Yes, I do very much and I am still learning to forgive myself.

Mr. Chui passed away over three decades ago, but he lives on forever in my heart. I occasionally catch myself talking to him in stressful times when I need someone to bounce ideas off of or just to listen to me, much the same way as I used to talk to him. He was gone too soon. As Mitch Albom writes in *Tuesdays with Morrie*, "Death is the end of a lifetime, not the end of a relationship."[1]

That night, Hu offered me the last two unsold cartons of Bois Chéri tea and asked me to never forget the store and to always remember the good old days, wherever I ended up.

I have since celebrated every milestone with a cup of this tea: my son's graduations, the births of my two boys, and my promotion to full professor. I dedicated my research award acceptance speech to him. Every morning, when I open the cupboard for my morning coffee, my eyes land on the Bois Chéri tea boxes. It gives

---

1. Mitch Albom, *Tuesdays with Morrie*, New York: Doubleday, p. 174.

me pause. The tea reminds me of the love, compassion, and blessings that I received from Mr. Chui and his family. I could not have achieved anything without his generosity, compassion, and blessings.

Many years later, while attending a Buddhist meditation, I was able to put into words Mr. Chui's actions towards others. I get disappointed and angry towards my boys who do not listen to my free advice. This is because there are expectations attached to my free advice. I buy them gifts to please them and if they don't reciprocate, I get frustrated and angry. Mr. Chui did not have any expectations of us. Instead, his kindness and compassion gave me space to learn about who I am and what I want to be. First, he advocated for me to have a Western education. Then he provided me with food and shelter while I went to school. Later, he gave me a moped which represented my freedom to move around without having to rely on others to pick me up or drop me off and not having to share the backseat of the van with cages of livestock.

Mr. Chui was my hero, role model, and everything. He taught me everything I needed to know in order to succeed. The direct or indirect messages I received from my interactions with him are do what you want to do, not what someone else tells you to do. And do not let anyone talk down to you.

Mr. Chui did not have any expectations for me to help in the store after school. He was just happy to see me hanging around. Even in my teenage years, when most young people prefer to hang out with their friends, I preferred to be at the store. I felt a sense of belonging when I was with the Chuis. Although I witnessed patience, compassion, kindness, and blessings in Mr. Chui's interactions with others, it is still a work in progress for me. I believe the power of relieving others from distress is like the lifeblood which is in all of us to give. Rachel Remen, a physician and author of *My Grandfather's Blessings* said, "When someone blesses you, it reminds you a little—untying the knots of belief and fear and self-doubt that have separated you from your own goodness."[2] It is like freeing you to give and receive blessings from everything around you. Mr. Chui's actions epitomized the giving and receiving of blessings.

2. Rachel Ramen, *My Grandfather's Blessings: Stories of Strength, Refuge, and Belonging.* New York: Riverhead Books, p. 12.

Chapter 8

LIFE AFTER HIGH SCHOOL

After I completed my High School Exams, I was in limbo. I did not know what to do with my life or where I was heading.

What I did know was that I did not have an excuse anymore to go to the tea store and that my daily routine was now drastically changed. My whole day was again spent attending to the various chores in the pagoda—it felt like an insult, now that I was "educated." Ah Pak would ask me to accompany her to pay visits to the sick or to go to town for groceries or supplies for the pagoda, but now I said no. I no longer enjoyed going into town with her in Ah Vee Ko or Mr. Fred's car. In fact, I would disassociate myself from her when she spoke loudly with merchants. She would ask for discounts with various merchants and when they refused, she would not take their no for an answer. I would pretend I did not know her as I was too embarrassed by her rudimentary knowledge of how things work.

Mauritius is a small island where everybody knows everybody. I vividly recall one particular incident when she tried to buy some incense from a superstore owned by the father of one of my classmates. The owner did not want to give her a discount for buying the incense in bulk. When I spotted my classmate in her father's store, I told Ah Pak that I was not feeling well and that I would wait for her in the car, whereupon I ran out of the store.

On our way back to the temple, I tried to explain the supply and demand curve; when the demand increases, the price increases as well and that the store needed to make money to cover the overhead. But it didn't matter as she felt I was not on her side. I told her that I did not want my classmate to tell other classmates that she was difficult.

I could see Ah Vee Ko listening in on our conversation and, from time to time, checking Ah Pak's reaction in the rear-view mirror. By the time we arrived at the pagoda she had figured out that I had only pretended to be sick in order to avoid embarrassment. This upset her and she did not allow me out of the temple for weeks.

The next time I was allowed to go to town was when Koung Koung was ill. I was sent to get cough syrup from the pharmacy on my moped. I took the opportunity to swing by the tea store to say hello to the Chui family. Mr. Chui was happy to see me and asked me why I had not been by. I told him that school was over and so I had to be at the pagoda to attend to all the various chores and even told him the story of getting into trouble with Ah Pak at the superstore, and my subsequent punishment.

"Ah," Mr. Chui said thoughtfully. "So that's why you haven't come to the store for weeks."

"It's not fair," I said.

"And then you explained basic economics to her!"

I did not understand why he was laughing.

"Remember, you are very lucky to have gone to school. Ah Pak has only had a grade three education in China. Perhaps you can find another way of getting her to understand your point of view?"

"But she is not a good listener and if she does not like something, she stops listening altogether. What will happen if the superstore decides to stop selling her incense because they are mad at her? Where will she buy incense to resell to the worshippers?"

"I don't think they will stop selling to her. She did not do anything wrong, other than argue with the owner about the price. But I see what you mean."

"Can you talk to her and make her understand that she is not to do it again? It is so embarrassing. I don't want to go in there with her again. My classmate's family owns the store. She will get a bad reputation on the island and when she enters the store nobody will want to serve her and she will not feel welcome!"

Mr. Chui just nodded.

I persisted. "Do you remember one of the merchants from Plaines des Papayes? Every time he came in, you all ignored him, but if I was around, I would serve the poor man! Do you know who I mean?"

"Yes, I know."

"Well, do you want Ah Pak to be treated like the merchant from Plaines des Papayes? Please talk with her. And also ask her not to punish me as she will know that I am the one who talked to you."

"I will see what I can do."

Mr. Chui's interest in this conversation was waning. He was more curious about how my applications to Canadian universities were coming along. I told him that I was still waiting. Maybe I was not good enough for any Canadian university to offer me an admission, I grumbled, and was doomed to stay in the pagoda for the rest of my life. "If I don't get accepted to a university, Ah Pak will never let me further my post-secondary education in Mauritius, not even taking secretarial courses. She will want me to stay in the pagoda to help her manage the place and take over when she becomes old." I could feel my emotions rising. It was both exhilarating and frightening to finally put words to all my fears. "I am getting too used to all my chores! I just mop the floors, water the plants, tend to the garden, work in the kitchen, and then spend the rest of the day just chanting and praying. I want more."

Mr. Chui listened intently—his attention was a balm— and asked me to be patient and not to give up. It was only July and universities had until September to send their offers. He told me that I was welcome to come to the store anytime I wanted, perhaps after attending to my chores in order to have a change of scenery. But my chores were never-ending, I told him. He suggested that if I worked well and fast, I could occasionally ask Ah Pak if I could visit his store.

It gave me hope.

Mr. Chui's suggestion worked even better than that. Very quickly, I found myself at the store almost every weekday for half a day regardless of whether I had finished my chores at the pagoda. I would take my moped and help Mr. Chui, Shu, Park and Heng. Every day they asked about my applications to Canadian universities and whether I had a Plan B in case I did not get an offer.

I asked Mr. Chui if he wanted to have the moped back, as Ah Pak was insisting that I return it. It has been parked in the pagoda courtyard most of the time and she was afraid that it would get stolen. Mr. Chui said that even though the employees could use an extra moped to do some errands, he preferred that I keep it so I could have a means of transportation to and from the pagoda. As well, he reminded me that the moped was registered in my name, although he was paying for its yearly insurance. And so, the moped stayed with me and even remained in the pagoda for a few more years after I had left Mauritius.

In addition to using the moped to and from the tea store, I would sometimes use it to carry Fen to pick up groceries. Some days I would take her just for a spin at the Champs de Mars racetrack. I would go full speed and she would hold on to me so tight that it was hard to breathe; then I would call her a *kapon*, meaning a scaredy cat. Every time she would say it was her last time riding with me, as I could not be trusted. But the next time I'd offer her a lift, she'd hop on. Towards, the end of my stay, she and I would go to buy snacks from local merchants in Plaine Verte, using the money that we received from Ah Pak for spring festivals or when we performed funeral rituals.

In any case, I did not always feel comfortable riding my moped alone. If Fen didn't join me, I would ask Lan or Ah Fi to come with me as I did not find it safe to cross Plaine Verte. There were several mosques on the road and, especially midday on Fridays, men of all ages congregated on the roads. They were not respectful and made comments and gestures that were difficult to ignore. It took me many years and some travelling before I could appreciate Muslim men, especially when they'd gather in numbers.

Ah Pak used to always remind us to be safe and told us stories of how women were raped and tortured in unsafe places. Mr. Chui would also remind me of safety rules, to be always cognizant of my surroundings and not to find myself in alleys or dark places, and that it was important that I get back to the pagoda before sunset.

Not much has changed in that regard. I am always aware of my surroundings, particularly when I am in unfamiliar places. To this day, I would not be going out at night in a new city or country alone. I would rather forgo the opportunity to visit or see a new place if I don't have a colleague or a friend to go with me.

Ah Feeti-Ah Pak in her coffin, a few days after her passing on September 11, 2021.

Ah Feeti-Ah Pak holding the author's first born, Jeremy, shortly after he was born.

Ah Feeti-Ah Pak and Stephanie Chitpin in Meixian, China, circa 1989.

Ah Feeti-Ah Pak giving a speech on the occasion of the 58th anniversary of the foundation of Fook Soo Am.

Ah Pak and the author with her sons Justin, left, and Jeremy in front of Fook Soo Am in 2013.

Stephanie Chitpin pays respect at Ah Feeti-Ah Pak's tomb at Nam Soon Cemetery in Port Louis, Mauritius, in May 2022.

Stephanie and her son Justin at Ah Feeti-Ah Pak's tomb, May 2022.

Ah Feeti-Ah Pak talking to François Woo at the ceremony for the 58th anniversary of the foundation of Fook Soo Am.

Stephanie Chitpin (right) and her friend Amélie at Loreto College, Port Louis, circa 1981.

Amélie, Stephanie and Isabelle in their uniforms at Loreto College.

Teacher Denise Chan Chak (second from left) with Amélie to her right, Isabelle and Stephanie, circa 1981.

Class photo at Loreto College, circa 1981.

Ah Feeti-Ah Pak surrounded by the nuns of Fook Soo Am: front row, left to right, Celine and Kaline; back row, Ah Khiook, Aline, Stephanie, Ah Pak, Fifi and Ah Shiong, circa 1989.

The author's son Justin in a private moment at Koung Koung's tomb at Bois Marchand Cemetery in Terre Rouge, Mauritius, in May 2022.

Jenny Fu, right, and a friend of hers. She died in a car accident circa 1981.

Tombstone of Koung Koung at
Bois Marchand Cemetery in
Terre Rouge, Mauritius.

Photo of Koung Koung
displayed at Fook Soo Am.

I was able to find Koung Koung's tomb at Bois Marchand
Cemetery in May 2022 to pay my respects to her finally.

Stephanie had a chance to return to Loreto College in May 2022.

The gates of Loreto College as seen in May 2022.

Mr. and Mrs. Chui, circa 1981.

Pow Koung, the author's favorite God at Fook Soo Am. He is the God of Justice.

Professor Leonard Adams, from the University of Guelph, and his wife Joyce visiting the author's apartment in Toronto, circa 1994.

Stephanie in front of the Ah Pak shrine at Fook Soo Am, in May 2022.

Chapter 9

MY FIRST INTERNSHIP

I have had an abiding interest in politics and law since as far back as I can remember. When I was completing my School Certificate, one of the regular worshippers at the Pagoda was running for office for the Mauritian Social Democrat Party (Parti Mauricien Social Démocrate, PMSD). I will honour his privacy, and so in this retelling, I shall call him Mr. Alexander.

Mr. Alexander was not fluent in Hakka and so he needed someone to act as an interpreter between him and Ah Pak. Soon after that, I volunteered to work on his electoral campaign. Ah Pak would not let me canvas door-to-door, so I was put to work writing the names of voters on flyers and other office duties. Back at the Pagoda, I shared Mr. Alexander's political platform with worshippers who were of voting age, spending hours convincing them to vote for PMSD and, if they did not have transportation, to let me know so I could arrange with Mr. Alexander's team to drive them to the polling stations. I kept a notebook with worshippers' names and addresses and their preferred pick-up times and communicated this information to Mr. Alexander so we could get out the vote.

I did all of these behind Ah Pak's back until one of the worshippers complained to her that I had become politically active and was adamant that future nuns should not be concerned with politics but with scriptures. I soon found myself having some explaining to do.

I was prepared for Ah Pak's question and had a list of reasons why the pagoda should support Mr. Alexander and his party. The pagoda would be more likely to get representation in the National Assembly, I told her. And when we were short of water, Mr. Alexander could call the fire station to have a tank of water delivered to us, particularly during celebrations such as the Chinese New Year or Buddha's Birthday. We could also have a police presence when we had big events to direct traffic and provide protection. I assured her that the pagoda would not have to pay for the police service if the request came from a government official. Ah Pak could not disagree with my explanations and that was the end of the argument.

On election day, the PMSD volunteer drivers stopped at the pagoda for refreshments, water or soda and whatever sweets Lan had made. Some of the drivers would also ask for water for their car radiator—Mauritius being a tropical country and because the coolant was not readily available, it was necessary to add water to the radiator to keep the car from overheating.

Unfortunately, Mr. Alexander was not elected but luckily, he was nominated by the party leader to serve as a Member of the Legislative Assembly as Minister of Justice. When he was in office, he supported the pagoda in various ways. He ensured that we had water and when there were big celebrations, he sent police officers to direct traffic and maintain order.

After Mr. Alexander was sworn in, his visits to the pagoda were more frequent. He would ask for Buddha's blessings and entreat Ah Pak to pray with him when faced with both personal and professional challenges. We became more familiar with each other as time passed. He thought I was smart and asked me one day how I had ended up living at the pagoda. I told him that I was Ah Pak's niece, claiming that she was my father's sister and that I had come to Mauritius when I was a baby—and left it at that.

Somewhere around this time, I needed to apply for a passport photo in anticipation of possibly travelling abroad should one of my university applications be successful. Mr. Chui referred me to a photo shop not far from his tea store to have my picture taken and said he would pay for it. However, before I could get a passport, I needed a birth certificate. I asked Ah Pak and she either told me that she did not have it or that she did not want to give it to me. I mustered enough courage and asked Mr. Alexander if he could help me get a copy.

"Where were you born, in Port Louis?" Mr. Alexander asked. "If so, it is not hard. The birth registrar is just across from my office."

The moment I always dreaded had arrived.

"Well ... I was born in Hong Kong."

Mr. Alexander was surprised. "This is more complicated, but not impossible. If you give me all the information, I should be able to help you."

I wrote down my birth date and my parents' names and my last name.

"How much will it cost?" I asked. "I am not sure I have enough money to pay for my birth certificate, but I can always do some clerical work for you.

Mr. Alexander kindly waved that suggestion away. "Don't worry about it. We can figure it out later.

And a couple of months later, he handed me my birth certificate and said that I owed him nothing. I was beyond grateful. I would have liked to leave it at that, but I still needed his help. When he later came to pray at the pagoda, I caught up with him by the water fountain where he was washing his hands. I asked him if he could help me get a passport application form from the British High Commission. Mr. Chui had been encouraging me for a long time to go to the British High Commission to get a passport application before I finished school, but I did not want to go for two reasons: firstly, the British High Commission closed at 2:30 p.m. and that would cut into my classes; secondly, I was a minor. It was better if the passport office clerks did not know who I was.

Mr. Alexander graciously told me that he could send his driver, Michael, to the British High Commission to get an application for me the next day. I walked him to his car and thanked him profusely. The driver started the engine but then Mr. Alexander told him to turn it off.

"Stephanie," he said, leaning out the window. "Does your Ah Pak know that you want to leave the pagoda?"

I hesitated. "Maybe."

"What do you mean by *maybe*? You are not trying to get me into trouble with Ah Pak, are you?

"No! I just don't know what to say or how to tell her. It's better I say nothing."

"Hmm. So, I help you get your passport and then you leave the pagoda without saying goodbye? I don't know if it is such a good idea for me to help you."

This was a terrible prospect. "No! Please don't worry. I will find a way of telling her my plans"

Mr. Alexander signalled to the driver to start the car again. "OK. I have your word. You'd better tell her."

He drove off and I spent that day revisiting all my conversations with Mr. Alexander, trying to discern whether I really had his support or not. I felt depressed and lost my appetite until, a few days later, Michael dropped off a passport application form at the pagoda. This got Ah Pak's attention.

Ah Pak had never met Michael so, when he asked to see me, she was immediately suspicious. How could there be a young man looking for me? I knew she would be thinking the worst: that he was my boyfriend. Mortified, I could hear her interrogate Michael from the next room.

"Mr. Alexander asked me to drop this off for Stephanie," Michael said.

"Who are you? What's inside the envelope?"

Afraid of his answers, I called out from the back room. "Mr. Alexander has sent some clerical work for me to do this evening." I am not sure where I came up with that lie.

Looking more favourably on the situation, Ah Pak asked Michael how long he and Mr. Alexander had known each other, how long he had been a driver, how are the roads, and so on, and gave him some tea. In this way, the conversation went in a different direction, and I was safe, at least for the time being. Later, Ah Pak asked me to tell her about the nature of the work I was doing for Mr. Alexander. I told her that it was political and confidential and that I was not at liberty to disclose any confidential information. Ah Pak looked at me suspiciously but, still in a relaxed mood, let me off the hook.

That night, I filled out the application and affixed Ah Pak's signature to the form, as I was a minor. I had a great deal of practice signing her name on various school forms. I went to Mr. Alexander's office the next day. His security guards wanted to stop me, but I told them that I was his goddaughter. I can't remember how much the birth certificate and the passport cost because Mr. Alexander offered to pay for my birth certificate and, if my memory serves me correctly, Mr. Chui paid for my passport.

A couple of weeks passed. One day Mr. Alexander showed up at the pagoda with an envelope containing my passport. "Here is your ticket to freedom," he said.

I was immensely grateful and of course, extremely excited. I held it close to my chest and took a deep breath before opening it. There, it was—my passport. I took it out of the envelope, turned each page, and stopped at the page with my picture and signature. For the very first time, the idea of leaving the pagoda and Mauritius was real. I hid it under my mattress so that no one could find it. Every night before I went to bed, I knelt beside my bed and prayed to Buddha to help me leave Mauritius. He answered my prayers when, one day, the offer of admission and an entrance scholarship from the University of Guelph for my bachelor's degree arrived.

I was too young to vote and to understand all the intricacies of politics. But I did know this much: PMSD was the only party not in favour of Mauritius getting its independence from Great Britain. At the time, I was a British subject and so, in an unconscious way, I did not want Mauritius to gain its independence as I would be considered a foreigner, not knowing at the time that the Mauritian Government had no record of me anyways. I was ignorant of the concept of colonialism both as a system and a practice. I supported PMSD without questioning its impact and its intentions.

Do I regret supporting Mr. Alexander and his party in retrospect? Categorically not. The time I spent volunteering on his campaign gave me life skills such as time management, organizational practices, and good communication. Do I share his party's ideology? Definitely not! My professional work speaks against it. Colonialism establishes dominance through power and authority. I am a product of its implementation and of struggles over the imposition of colonial educational curricula in Mauritius, where I was taught more about things outside my vicinity than those in my own backyard. But I digress.

Chapter 10

MY FIRST FRIEND

I was fourteen years old when I met Jenny Fu at the pagoda during the celebrations of the Buddha's birthday. She was my first friend. Good-natured, kind and thoughtful, she was Taiwanese and was working in a textile factory in Mauritius. Jenny was coming to the pagoda every other week to offer up prayers for her parents' health. She spoke Mandarin and some English, so I was the interpreter between her and Ah Pak. We hit it off well. Every Friday after work, I would pick her up on my moped so we could spend the whole weekend together. Best of all, I was allowed to share one of the guest rooms with her. She would always bring us some fancy food such as chocolate, cookies, or Perrier water. I had never seen bubbly water prior to knowing her. After lunch on Sundays, I dropped her off at her place.

Despite our age difference—Jenny was in her early thirties—I confided in her about my dream to leave the pagoda and Ah Pak. We would spend all night coming up with scenarios of how I could make this happen. Jenny was always supportive of my dreams and wishes.

We mostly spoke English among ourselves so none of the nuns would know what we were plotting.

I also shared some of my nightmares, such as one that was provoked by a traumatic event that occurred when I was eight years old. Specifically, an Asian taxi driver was brutally murdered and his body was recovered in the trunk of the taxi in a badly mutilated state. The body was exposed in an open casket. That night when the family asked Ah Pak to perform the ritual, I had to fill in for Lan who was sick with the flu. When someone is dead, there are always three nuns that perform the ritual; I was thus compelled to accompany Ah Pak and Fen. Police were everywhere when we arrived at the Kit Lock Funeral Home. With the casket just a couple of feet away from the altar where the three of us were standing, I could not help but see the deceased's mutilated face.

That night when I finally fell asleep, I had nightmares and woke up screaming for help at the top of my lungs. It was so loud that I awoke Koung Koung, who thought I was possessed by demons and spirits. Koung Koung said that the deceased was seeking justice for being brutally murdered and was trying to communicate his desires for justice to me. Koung Koung also asked Ah Pak not to take me to perform future funeral rituals, as I was too young.

Jenny taught me some Mandarin and encouraged me to apply to Taipei University. She reasoned that if I were to study Buddhism in Taiwan, Ah Pak would approve. Once there, I could transfer to a university in Canada. In the meantime, she suggested that I enroll in correspondence accounting courses while waiting for an offer of admission. She suggested that an acquaintance of hers, Alfred, could tutor me through the course on Sunday mornings. Having planted the seed in my head, I asked Mr. Chui if he would pay for me to enroll in an accounting correspondence course based in the UK. He agreed to speak to Ah Pak and, shortly after, I was enrolled in the correspondence courses.

This is how Alfred became my first tutor. Alfred wore spectacles and had a moustache, and was respect- ful, intelligent, and comical, finding funny stories to illustrate the concepts of debits and credits, assets and liabilities. I completed three modules under Alfred's guidance. He arrived at the pagoda every Sunday mor- ning and we spent all morning reviewing the course materials and checking my work before I mailed it back for scoring. I was doing well and enjoying the courses.

During this time, I also had a chance to practice my English with both Jenny and Alfred. I enjoyed their company very much until late one Thursday evening in February.

Jenny would usually call me at the end of the week to confirm when I was to pick her up. Because of her supervisory role, she would not know far in advance if meetings or deadlines would keep her late. Mostly, I picked her up late afternoon so she could join us for dinner. One Friday, it was getting late and I still had not heard from her. I called the factory and was trans- ferred to many people, each one putting me on hold. Finally, her boss came on the phone and told me that Jenny had been involved in a car accident the night before and was at the Civil Hospital. He gave me no more information.

Ah Pak came with me. We headed out right away. We arrived shortly after 6 p.m. and had trouble finding out where she might be. Finally, a doctor overheard us asking yet another nurse and pointed us in the direction of the morgue. Ah Pak held my hand. "Let's go home and maybe ask Mr. Alexander to speak with the hospital official tomorrow," she said softly.

"No," I said. "I need to know where my friend is and I am not going home until I find Jenny."

We gave Jenny's name to the nurse at the morgue.

"Are you related to the patient?" she asked us.

By then my emotions were getting the better of me. "She is my best friend and I need to see how she is doing!"

The nurse asked if she could speak with Ah Pak privately. But as Ah Pak did not speak Creole, we were told to come back with an adult who spoke Creole and who could translate.

I told her that I was the goddaughter of the Minster of Justice. I could give my godfather a call and she could let him know what ward Jenny was in and about her condition. This finally convinced the nurse to speak to me.

She touched my shoulder and said, "I did not want to give you the sad news. Your friend is in the morgue, waiting for her family to identify her body. The man with her, Alfred, has also died. I am so sorry."

She explained that they had been in a horrific accident involving two lorries and a taxi on the highway. According to the police report, the taxi veered off the road to avoid an animal and crashed into an oncoming lorry, and then a second lorry crashed into the first. Jenny and Alfred had been on their way back from the wedding of one of their colleagues.

I collapsed.

I woke up in my bed, heavily sedated.

Ah Pak let me sleep with her that night, consoling me as I woke up from nightmare after nightmare. For the first time, I saw a different Ah Pak; instead of being stern and matter of fact, she was being caring and motherly. I fell ill with a fever and a cough, and so stayed in her room for the next few days. I was not given any medication, nor was I provided with any counselling for my grief. Despite Ah Pak's gentleness, I grieved on my own and, in the process, I lost quite a few pounds and had to miss school.

Because of my illness, I was not allowed to attend Jenny and Alfred's funerals, which was held for them jointly. Ah Pak and Fen attended their cremations in my place. Alfred's wife travelled from Taiwan with their young daughter to attend the service and take back his ashes. Other than the workers in the factory who attended, Ah Pak and Fen were the only people to represent Jenny. I knew Jenny's parents were alive, but it was a mystery why they did not attend her funeral. She never told me anything about them, or even whether she had siblings.

Coincidentally, the last weekend that Jenny spent at the pagoda, she had asked to sleep in the bedroom I shared with Koung Koung instead of the guest room. There was a wooden desk and a chair by my bed where

I did my schoolwork. She sat on the chair and showed me how to write her name in Chinese. As an example, she wrote out her parents' names and address.

Several months after her death I was slowly recovering and coming to terms with the fact that I had lost my two good friends. One of the things that carried me through this period was the story that Ah Pak used to tell me about the young prince, Buddha. On his secret nightly walks, he saw sick people, old people, homeless people, people in pain and people dying. He discovered that life itself is a form of suffering. The rich who come to pray suffer because of their riches, while the poor suffer because of their poverty. People without a family suffer because we don't have a family, and people who do have a family suffer because of their family. Those who pursue worldly pleasures suffer because of their indulgences, and those who abstain from worldly pleasures suffer because of their abstention. We all suffer, though not all suffering is equal.

Soon after I got better, a group of Taiwanese sailors came to pray. We occasionally saw sailors of various Asian nationalities stopping by, as Port Louis is a seaport. I usually did not have much to do with sailors, as they were chauvinistic and condescending. This time, however, one of the Taiwanese sailors, a middle-aged man, was a gentleman and treated me quite respectfully when I sold him the incense.

After he did his prayers, I offered him a cup of tea and some sweets and asked him in English if he would help me locate some people in Taiwan. He said that he would, except that Taiwan is much bigger than Mauritius and that it might be more challenging. I showed him Jenny's parents' names and address. He offered to help me write a letter to them. I was thrilled.

I went to the post office and had the letter registered so that I could know when it was delivered. A few months later, I heard back from Jenny's parents. I could not read it so took it to Heng to read it for me.

The letter was written by Jenny's younger sister, Jin. She thanked me for reaching out and described the struggles they faced in claiming Jenny's ashes, her death insurance benefits, and her personal belongings. Jin shared how devastated their parents were. I learned for the first time that Jenny had come to work in Mauritius in order to be able to provide for her whole family. Upon hearing the news, I was more angry than sad. I called up Mr. Alexander and asked if I could meet with him in his office. I shared the whole story with him and asked him to find a way to help Jenny's family.

Mr. Alexander was busy but seemed moved by the story. "What do you want me to do?"

I asked if he could find out where Jenny's ashes were, as well as track down her life insurance policy. I gave him all the information I had and even asked if he could set up a meeting to meet with the owner of the textile manufacturer where she had been working. He agreed to try all this.

Mr. Alexander did not speak much Hakka and I did not speak any Mandarin. Most of the Asians working in Mauritius spoke Mandarin and so there was definitely a language barrier, not to mention that many of our exchanges were lost in translation. Not much happened for a while, until one day Mr. Alexander let me know that he had set up an appointment for us to speak with Jenny's boss. Michael came to pick me up at the pagoda and I wore my best outfit, even borrowing Shu's high-heeled sandals to look taller and older. The night before, I could not sleep as I rehearsed over and over what I wanted to say to Jenny's boss.

At the meeting, Mr. Alexander did not mince his words. He asked that Jenny's ashes and belongings be returned to her family. The next item was her life insurance policy. I was too young to understand all the intricacies, but towards the end of the meeting, Mr. Alexander asked me if I had anything to add. I told Mr. Lee, the owner of the factory, that I expected him to do the right thing by complying with our requests and to let my friend, Jenny, rest in peace.

Things moved slowly from there. A full year passed when finally, Mr. Alexander informed me that Jenny's ashes and 50,000 Hong Kong Dollars of life insurance benefits had been sent to her parents. I broke down in tears and thanked Mr. Alexander for all his help and told him that good karma would always follow him and that he would always have Buddha's blessings.

Despite this, I had a nagging question: what if the parents did not receive her ashes and the insurance money? How would I ever find out the truth? There was still no closure for me.

A few years later, Ah Pak's mother passed and when she had collected enough donations she planned a trip, her first, to Meixian, China, for the memorial service. I asked Mr. Chui if I could work for him to earn enough money to buy myself a return ticket to accompany her. I told him that as Ah Pak did not speak Creole, nor did she know how to read and write, she needed someone to accompany her. Mr. Chui offered to pay for my airfare and, a few days before our departure, he even gave me some extra cash for emergencies.

Ah Pak was not the least bit surprised when I told her that I would be her travel companion on her trip to the Far East. She told me that I was a lucky girl as few had the opportunity to travel by air. She particularly liked the fact that I would get to learn about Chinese culture, as she believed that my Western education had compromised my views of Chinese customs and traditions. I did not disagree with her openly, as I wanted to be respectful of her views.

I was never good at geography and so I went to our school library to research Meixian and Kaohsiung City. I found out that there would be some extra costs if I was to travel to Jenny's parents and sister. I mustered up more courage and went to Mr. Chui and asked if he thought it would be a good idea to travel from Meixian and Kaohsiung City to visit the Fus. I told him that it would bring me closure if I knew that they had in fact received Jenny's ashes and death benefits. He asked me to run my ideas past Ah Pak.

One day I caught Ah Pak in a good mood and shared my plan. She looked at me pensively. "Where do you think we will find money for transportation from Meixian to Kaohsiung? I understand that it will bring you the closure that you need, but I think you are asking for trouble."

I caught myself responding without thinking: "I can work for Mr. Chui at his store if you let me leave the pagoda for three days a week."

Surprisingly, Ah Pak agreed. For the next little while I worked two shifts, one at the pagoda and one at the tea store, until I saved enough money to pay for both of our return train tickets from Meixian to Kaohsiung.

We travelled to China, via first Bombay (Mumbai) and then Hong Kong. We had a full day layover in Hong Kong, which I was excited about. This is where you were born, Ah Pak reminded me, in a rare moment of the acknowledgment of my origins.

Hong Kong was even more incredible and beautiful than I imagined. An endless landscape of modern skyscrapers against a backdrop of verdant mountains. When one looked closer there were also older buildings and narrow alleys and Chinese neon signs, hinting of an earlier era. With its mix of both east and west, and its seamless blend of British and Asian, Hong Kong was so different from Mauritius and everything I knew. Everything moved and everyone was in a hurry. I didn't know exactly how, but I knew that had I been raised in Hong Kong my life would be very different today.

It took us a whole day to get from Hong Kong to Meixian and we got there just in time for the memorial service. Finally, the day came. After the memorial services in Meixian, Ah Pak and I travelled to Kaohsiung, Taiwan. As promised, Ah Pak was taking me to Jenny's family.

We met Jin in our hotel room on our second night in Kaohsiung. I gave her a calculator that Jenny had given me and that I had treasured as a reminder of her. Jin did not look anything like Jenny, but was much shorter with smaller eyes, long black hair and thin lips. She must have been just a couple of years older than me. She spoke some English and so we managed to converse. I learned that her family had to use most of Jenny's life insurance for her father's medical care and that she had to quit school to enter the workforce to support her family. Tears rolled down my cheeks when she shared these sad stories with us. She invited us to meet her parents the following night and asked if they could send us a taxi. We did not accept her offer of transportation, as I still had some of the money that Mr. Chui gave me to buy food for the memorial service. I told Jin that we would accept their kind invitation to meet her parents and that we would be happy to find our own way to her apartment.

As agreed, we showed up after dinner. We were greeted warmly and were seated at their kitchen table. Mrs. Fu offered us tea and cookies and we could immediately sense that they were not in a good place. Jin acted as our intermediary as the parents did not speak any English. The three of them lived in a small one-bedroom apartment. From the kitchen, we could see a mattress lying on the floor of their bedroom. Mr. Fu hardly said anything as he was quite ill and weak. Mrs. Fu held my hands several times and bowed. I bowed back and asked Jin to thank her parents for receiving us in their home. Mrs. Fu told us that Jenny had started working for the textile manufacturer in Taiwan when she turned 16 and had been promoted to

KEEP MY MEMORY SAFE

a supervisory role when she turned 25. The business was booming and the owner decided to open another factory in Mauritius. Jenny was asked if she would like to help the company set up in Mauritius. Mrs. Fu asked how I had met Jenny and how she was doing prior to her death. I recounted my interactions with Jenny as truthfully as I could and as Ah Pak did not understand any English, I was free to share how I had sought Jenny's advice about leaving the pagoda. Both Mrs. Fu and Jin smiled and thought I was quite an adventurous girl.

That night, when we got back to the hotel, I took stock of all the good things that were happening in my life and how fortunate I was to be fed, to have a roof over my head and a bed to sleep in every night. I thanked Ah Pak profusely for allowing me to get an education. Often we discover the place in us that carries the light only after it has become dark. Sometimes it is only in the dark that we know the value of this place. I was thankful for everything I had been given. I felt privileged to have known Jenny. She will always be my friend and we will meet someday again.

Chapter 11

LEAVING MAURITIUS

It was early August when the offer of the scholarship arrived. Every afternoon, I would wait for the postman, listening for the bicycle bell ringing from afar. Every day I asked him how long it took for mail to get to Mauritius from Toronto, Canada. Every day he said it was something like three weeks to a month.

He knew not to leave my mail with the other nuns. I was suspicious that Ah Pak and Fen would intercept it and find out that I was leaving the pagoda. They still did not know anything about my plans.

Every day he greeted me with, "No mail for you today, Miss."

Until one day he handed me an envelope. Return address: Canada. I ran inside and hid it, only opening it later, in the dark, after everyone had gone to sleep. It almost felt like the scholarship was glowing in the dark.

Now it was time to apply for my student visa. There were so many hoops to jump through and requirements to meet. One of them was to provide financial statements from my parents, guardians, or sponsor. Mr. Chui not only offered to pay for any fees associated with my studies, he also volunteered to sponsor me. He instructed me to see his accountant, Jeffrey Ng, who had just returned to Mauritius after finishing his studies in the UK. He was looking for a job and it was hard at that time for young professionals to find work, most of the businesses preferring to hire someone with experience. Nevertheless, Mr. Chui hired him as his accountant. A couple of days before my visa interview, I went to see Jeffrey at his office and asked to have Mr. Chui's financial statements. He seemed surprised to see me.

"Who are you? What's your name? Are you his granddaughter?"

"I am Seymoye," I said, using the name the Chui family called me, along with the nuns in the temple. It meant little girl in Hakka and was my nickname. Even to this day, I am still called Seymoye by the Chuis, Fen and Lan.

"How are you related to Mr. Chui?"

"I don't know," I said, and meant it.

But Jeffrey was suspicious. "I am not going to give you Mr. Chui's financial statements. Who told you to come and see me?"

"Mr. Chui instructed me to see you! I need the financial statements for tomorrow, as I have my interview with the Canadian Immigration Officer."

"What does your interview have anything to do with Mr. Chui's financial statements? I am not going to give them to you."

He was getting exasperated, but so was I. "You are leaving me no choice but to tell Mr. Chui that you are uncooperative. He might have to retain the services of another accountant."

Jeffrey looked at me angrily and proceeded to call the tea store to speak with Mr. Chui. I could see that Mr. Chui was confirming my story. Jeffrey looked at me, shook his head and rolled his eyes.

"You can come back tomorrow to pick up the statements," was all he said as he brusquely showed me the door.

Mauritius did not have a Canadian embassy, so the fastest way of obtaining a student visa was to visit the embassy in Nairobi. Once a year, a representative from the Canadian Immigration Office comes to Mauritius to issue visas to those who could not travel to Nairobi. It was thus late in August that I was finally granted an interview with Canadian Immigration.

My appointment was on a Wednesday at the Royal Palm Beachcomber Luxury Hotel in Grand-Baie. Mr. Alexander's driver, Michael, drove me in his BMW. The entrance of the hotel was magnificent, with beautiful orchids and roses lining the way. It was my first experience of a resort hotel and I was overwhelmed by the beauty around me. I never knew that Mauritius was more than the sun, the sky and the sea—and lots of dust and dirt. I walked up to the reception desk and asked for Mr. Baker. A young woman took me to the meeting room where I was met by a middle-aged man.

Mr. Baker looked at me and then at the picture in my passport, as if unsure how to proceed. He read aloud the offer of scholarship at the University of Guelph. He asked me what my parents did for a living, where I lived in Port Louis, and who would be paying for my living expenses. I told him everything and handed him Mr. Chui's financial statements.

He scanned every page, pouring over it all. Then he put them down on his desk and looked at me for a long time. "You are a lucky girl. I would have terminated your interview right here without these papers."

He asked me several questions about Canada and also tested my fluency in English. He thought that I had some kind of a British accent. He commented on my education at the Loreto Convent. He shared my fascination with Canada having two official languages, French and English, which is quite similar to Mauritius, whose official language is English but French and Creole are widely spoken throughout the island. I drew his attention to all the advertisements around the resort written in both English and French. I told him that the more I read about Canada, the more I was interested in this beautiful, multicultural country. I was particularly drawn to their former Prime Minister, Pierre Trudeau, on account of his charisma, intellect, and personality.

By that time, I was quite at ease with Mr. Baker. I told him that I admired Prime Minister Trudeau's personal motto, Reason Before Passion, and that I had read how his policies had received polarizing reactions across Canada. I followed the stories in the news that he was able to maintain national unity in the face of the Quebec sovereignty movement and that he had also fostered a pan-Canadian identity. Most of all,

I admired Mr. Trudeau's intellect and political acumen. But mostly, because Canada's two official languages were languages that I was fluent in, Canada was my country of choice.

Mr. Baker seemed to enjoy my conversation, and after an hour he stamped my passport and sent me off with his best wishes.

I walked out of the resort feeling numb and disoriented. The import of what I had just done—guaranteeing my escape—was starting to hit me. I somehow found the parking lot but forgot where the car was. I stood in the middle of the hot asphalt for long minutes before I heard my name: "Stephanie, over here."

Michael was waving over rows of car roofs. He held open the door for me and asked how my interview had gone. I told him that I was both sad and happy. Sad that I would be leaving all of them, but happy that I was given a chance to begin a new chapter of my life. I was anxiously looking forward to it. He was so happy for me that he offered to buy me a pastry at one of the best-known pastry shops on the island. I chose a lemon tart and I asked him to drop me off at Mr. Chui's store.

When Mr. Chui saw the red BMW car in front of the store, he came out and told Michael that there was no need to wait for me as Park would take me back to the pagoda. Once inside, I told Mr. Chui, Shu, Heng and Park that I had successfully secured my student visa. They were all happy for me. There were many smiles, but also a heavy silence, a quietness of disbelief or shock. And sadness.

My whole month of August was spent running errands. Shu suggested that I get warm sweaters, a pair of jeans, some undergarments, and a couple of pairs of socks, as I would be living in a cold country. It was hard to believe that one would have to wear so many clothes.

As always, I did my chores and even got up a couple of hours earlier to do some of Lan or Fen's chores. I knew I was leaving them behind for good, and I felt guilty that the special treatment that was being given to me by Ah Pak and the Chuis had opened up a world of possibilities that they would never experience. I would not have to be a nun like them.

As for Ah Pak, she still had no idea that I was leaving. It was a stressful time, as I just did not know what to say to her, not only because I knew she would be sad, but I was afraid that she might call on the authorities to report my forging her signature on my passport application. The Chui family agreed that we should not inform Ah Pak of my leaving, as they too were afraid of the consequences.

I told Koung Koung of my plan. She was the only one to gently insist that I tell Ah Pak, suggesting that Sunday dinner would be the best time. At the end of the meal, as we were giving thanks, I took a deep breath.

"I also want to send my heartfelt thanks to Buddha for answering my prayers for obtaining a scholarship at a Canadian University." I looked in Ah Pak's direction and added, "This means that I will be leaving the pagoda very soon. In two days, actually."

She looked up quickly and didn't say anything for a full minute. I could see her mind working through the information as her body sat stock-still in shock. Finally, tears began to stream down her cheeks. She was happy for me, she said, but how could I leave her behind? And who will take care of the mail and bills?

I reassured her that Mr. Chui and Park would help and that she would not notice any difference. I told her I would find a part-time job to support myself and promised that I would write every week—in Chinese with the help of a dictionary. I looked around the table. Fen and Lan were quiet, and Koung Koung's cheeks were glistening wet. I wondered if she was the saddest. "Nobody will look after me when I am sick," she said. "I will probably die soon."

I hugged her and told her that both Fen and Lan would look after her and they loved her as much as I did. The five of us stayed at the dinner table until almost bedtime, something we had never done. It was the most family-feeling time I ever remember experiencing at the pagoda.

I continued to perform all my chores and also tried to spend as much time at the tea store as possible. I was even allowed to stay out later. I promised Mr. Chui that I would do my very best to make him proud.

On the morning of my departure, Park showed up with an old suitcase. It was big and my clothes floated inside it. Koung Koung offered to give me a wool blanket that she kept in her trunk to take back to her family in China one day. I hesitated and then accepted the kind gift. The blanket filled my suitcase and reminded me of her. It would keep me warm for years, staying with me only until a fire claimed my home in Ottawa in 2015.

Lan wrapped a few rice cakes and other sweets and savouries for me to take along. Ah Pak and Fen rummaged in the wardrobe that we all shared to find items that they could gift me. Fen found an old black T-shirt, and Ah Pak offered me one of her cardigans. I felt very blessed with all the gifts that I was receiving.

I rode my moped for the last time to the tea store and spent the afternoon serving clients. I said goodbye to the Chuis and all the employees, and I also thanked Ah Yan who had driven me to and from the pagoda when I was living with the Chuis. I hugged and kissed Mr. Chui and thanked him for all his gifts and blessings. I told him that I loved him and would miss him very much. There were tears in his eyes, and he hugged me without saying a word. It was the first time I witnessed Mr. Chui being emotional in all the years that I had known him.

Back at the pagoda, I parked my moped at the top of the stairs by the kitchen and said goodbye to it. I handed the key to Ah Pak and asked her to take care of it while I was away. She put it inside the wardrobe and promised that I would find it in the same place when I came back after my studies. I shared a last meal with all the nuns. We could hardly swallow anything as we were overcome with emotion. I thanked Buddha, Pow Koung Low Yah and all of them for their blessings.

Mr. Chui had asked Park to purchase the most direct flight from Mauritius to Canada. Park found me the cheapest fare at Atom Travel for September 8. I was to fly from Mauritius to Johannesburg to Heathrow, and finally to Toronto.

I left Mauritius on a Tuesday, a week after the start of classes. Mr. Alexander invited Ah Pak and Fen to ride with us to the airport. It normally takes approximately an hour to get to the airport from Port Louis, but on that night, everything seemed to be going faster. Mr. Alexander broke the silence by asking me if I had made any arrangements for someone to pick me up in Guelph and whether I would be living in the residence. I told him that I was in touch with one of my professors who was kind enough to help me find a room in somebody's house not far from the university, and that I would have only two kilometres to walk to school. He thought I was resourceful and wanted me to share this news with Ah Pak. It seemed to quiet her mind, knowing that I had a place to live and that I would be safe.

At the airport, Mr. Alexander parked in the VIP section, which meant I did not have to go through customs right away. Everyone waited with me in the lounge until it was time to board the plane. Then someone looked at their watch and we hugged and said goodbye one last time.

I walked out of the VIP lounge directly onto the tarmac. The plane was parked a few hundred metres away. I looked around me but there was no Ah Pak. I realized that for the first time in my life I was very much alone.

The flight attendant closed the door and within minutes the plane began its taxiing. Then it abruptly stopped. The captain announced that they had found a missing item belonging to one of the passengers.

Suddenly, Mr. Alexander was rushing down the aisle looking for me. I could not believe my eyes.

"What are you doing here?"

"I forgot to give you the camera!" He was out of breath. "We were going to the car when Jane pointed out your camera hanging on my neck."

He hung it around my neck and began sprinting back the way he came. "Bon voyage and let us know when you get to Canada!"

As the plane prepared to move again, I looked out the window. Mr. Alexander was on the tarmac with Ah Pak, Fen, Jane and others, all waving. I fought the urge to jump up and ask the flight attendant to let me off. But I was too late, the plane was suddenly in the air.

I fell asleep shortly after take-off. When I woke up at 2 a.m. Mauritian time, my seating partner told me that she was travelling to London to visit her daughter. I began to hear Creole spoken all around; the plane was full of Mauritians. The familiarity was comforting. Little had changed other than the scenery. We landed at Johannesburg at 4 a.m., local time, and had a layover of 14 hours ahead. I visited all the shops at the airport and spent time going through the books and magazines at Coles bookstore. I couldn't stop thinking about Lan and Fen, who were doing my chores in addition to theirs, and how lucky I was to leave the pagoda. I passed the time sitting in the waiting lounge, blissfully idle and napping. At one point, I noticed that someone had left a book behind. It was *Their Eyes Were Watching God* by Zora Neale Hurston. I moved to that chair in case someone returned for it and opened it up. It kept me company for the next six hours as I read it from cover to cover.

Finally, it was time to board for Heathrow and I was assigned another window seat. My partner was a White South African who did not say a word and did his best to ignore me when I asked if I could please go to the restroom. I kept the cookies, water and roll of bread for later in my backpack and slept with an eye open as I did not trust my seating partner. At Heathrow, I followed the directions to Air Canada and was happy to note that the layover was only a couple of hours.

I was getting closer to my final destination.

On the flight to Toronto, I kept on looking at my watch, given to me by Mr. Chui for my tenth birthday. I seldom wore it but put it on for this journey. I had been travelling for almost two days. When we landed at Pearson Airport, I could not wait to disembark.

After getting through customs, I ran out of the airport, mesmerized. The sky was so big, and people were everywhere, many of them seemingly in a rush. Everything was orderly and clean, and the taxis were all lined up so nobody had to fight to get into one. I followed the queue and a gentleman a few steps ahead of me said, "Go ahead, Miss."

I thanked him and took the next cab to the Toronto Coach Terminal on Bay Street. Once there, I bought a single ticket and boarded the coach that took me to the University of Guelph.

It was September the 10th when I showed up at my room and board. A young man opened the door and invited me in. His mother, Mrs. Estrada, showed me to my room in the basement of the house. In it was a single bed, a desk and a chair, and an old wardrobe for me to store my clothes. It was everything. A new chapter in my life had begun.

Chapter 12

BEGINNINGS IN CANADA

I had never heard of the concept of a basement prior to living in one. With no window in the bedroom, it did not take long to fall deeply asleep. The next morning was a fine day, with a sliver of sun shining brightly through the bathroom window. A perfect morning to start my new life in a new country.

My watch was still set to Mauritian time. I wondered what Mr. Chui, Park, the nuns, and particularly Ah Pak and Koung Koung, would be doing now. I sat down at my desk and wrote to Mr. Chui and Ah Pak on the paper I had gotten from one of the flights, and told them everything about my journey so far, and what my plans were for the day. I promised to write them by the end of the week with more news. Despite a hectic student life, I kept this promise throughout my undergraduate years.

The next thing I missed was my moped. I had to walk to the university. Instead of complaining about it—not that there was anyone to complain to—I tried to think of walking and carrying groceries as exercise, seeing as I no longer had to scrub the floors or wash the cups.

On my first day, I stopped at the University Centre in order to register for my courses. The international student advisor explained how it all worked and what I would need to take as a full-time student. They were all mandatory or prerequisite courses, and I was able to fit two additional French courses into the timetable. I registered under my birth name, Oi-chu Shiu Fook Sien.

When I saw that I had back-to-back classes on Mondays and Tuesdays, I made the decision to finally set my watch to Toronto time. It felt like a momentous gesture, an acceptance that I was moving another step away from the people I left behind. Tears ran down my cheeks as the time moved forward on my wrist.

My Introduction to Sociology class was in a big lecture hall packed with almost four hundred students. I felt lost and wondered how my professor would remember all our names. We were introduced to our teaching assistants and were told that, if we needed help, we could reach out to them. By the end of class, I realized that the professor was there just to give his lecture and that the teaching assistants were like tutors.

Most of my courses were in lecture halls, except for my two French courses. I did not make any friends in my first semester. In fact, I did not make any friends during my university years at Guelph. My natural reticence coupled with a desperate need to succeed—indeed, I did not feel like I had a choice; people in my position rarely do—meant that I had little time and even less inclination to be social. Even so, I was happy to finally be able to pursue my dream of receiving a post-secondary education.

My professors were courteous and friendly, yet distant. They were available by appointment to speak with you on matters relating to the course, but nothing else. I noticed right away that Professor Adams was different.

He was of African descent, middle-aged, and looked exactly how I imagined a professor would look. When he found out I was an international student, he asked how I liked the university and offered to take me on a tour of the campus. He was curious why I was taking a heavy load of seven courses in my first semester. I shared my plan of finishing my degree quickly to save money.

"You know you can take three years to complete your Bachelors so long as you maintain an A- average in all of your courses," he told me. "The university will pay your tuition fees for up to three years. But by taking so many courses, you might be compromising your chances of obtaining an A- average at the end of the semester. You can always drop the courses that you do not like before the deadline."

I was skeptical and could only think of ways to secure my financial stability. "Do you know if anyone at the university needs help with clerical work?"

"No, not really. You mean doing filing, answering telephone calls?"

"Yes, anything that would allow me to be financially independent."

He shook his head. "You are a foreign student; you are not entitled to work. Besides, you have a full load of courses. I would not advise you to take on a part-time job. May I ask what your parents do for a living?"

I told him about my situation, and that Mr. Chui was paying my room and board and other expenses.

He looked surprised and apologized for asking personal questions. "How do you like your living arrangement?"

"I have my own room for the first time in my life." I smiled.

Again, he looked surprised but did not ask me to elaborate. "And where are you buying your groceries?"

I told him that I would pick up a loaf of bread, margarine and a couple cans of beans at the Quickies, but that I found the food quite expensive.

"Yes, it is expensive if you buy it at the convenience stores. Let me give you the addresses of Zellers and Giant Tiger. The food is much cheaper if you buy it in a supermarket." We left his office and he showed me how to take the bus from the campus to Zellers and Giant Tiger.

We did not see each other again until a few weeks later as I was busy with various assignment deadlines. However, I gave some serious thought to his advice to take three years to finish my degree. When I got a B+ in my first assignment, I attempted to seek the counsel of my psychology professor as to whether I should drop his course. Although he made time to speak with me and was polite, he let me know quickly that his role as a professor was to teach and not to counsel students, as the university had counsellors to do just that. In the end, I decided to stick with the seven courses and see how well I did before the course withdrawal deadline.

I caught up with Professor Adams one afternoon at the University Centre. I told him that I was doing well and, as a matter of fact, I had gotten three of the four assignments back and they were all in the A- range. He was happy for me and asked me to keep up the good work. He then said: "You will need to get a winter coat. Your t-shirt and cardigan are not enough to keep you warm. We have lots of snow here. You can find some clothes at Zellers. If you need help, I can ask my wife to help you pick out a winter coat and a pair of winter boots." It felt like odd advice, but I thanked him and said that I could take care of it.

The course taught by my sociology professor, the late Ian Currie, was one of the most captivating. He was a parapsychologist with a special interest in de-hauntings. He would tell us that people called him as a last resort. In his class, we would be sitting quietly and attentively and whenever we heard a noise, we would literally scream. It was at times both funny and scary. It was hard not to feel jumpy when he shared with us his psychic insight and abilities and recounted stories of frightened house owners seeking his help.

"Ghosts are lingering spirits," he said once, "who, for one reason or another, refuse to accept that they are dead and are sometimes reluctant to leave the premises they once occupied and felt attached to. Often, all the ghosts need is a sympathetic push to cross to the other realm but, sometimes, even with the best efforts, they do not want to be pushed."

I raised my hand and asked about techniques used to de-haunt a house or speak to the dead. He described the different categories of hauntings, such as delusional ones, when we hear noises in the attic, and how most often it is just squirrels. In contrast, there are the poltergeists, which involve objects flying around. Professor Currie further added that, "With poltergeists, there is usually an adolescent in the house and there is a lot of kinetic energy which has nothing to do with the dead." There were hardly any absences in his class, as we all looked forward to learning more ghost stories.

Meanwhile, I had been channelling all of my energy into my studies and budgeting and managing my monthly expenses. I was also responsible for my own food. I would take a couple of hours on Saturday to prepare my meals for the week, as I was allowed to use Mrs. Estrada's kitchen and store my food in their fridge. I had never cooked before as Lan was in charge of all the meals at the pagoda. She would make us stir fry vegetables of various sorts from the garden and serve them with steamed or fried rice. Our protein was from tofu. At that time, food items such as tofu were not readily available in Guelph supermarkets, and I had to substitute other grains for protein. I would make steamed rice that I stir fried with soy sauce. Fresh vegetables were expensive for my meagre budget, so I would buy cans of peas, corn, kidney beans or chickpeas. I would have rice for dinner, and for lunch I had two slices of bread with margarine, a banana and a thermos of instant coffee. I thought of Lan every time I cooked and even tried to guess what she would add to the rice if she did not have the vegetables from the garden. I graduated to peanut butter sandwiches for the next few months. I had never tried peanut butter before but instantly fell in love with it. One morning, I saw my landlord preparing a peanut butter *and jam* sandwich for her son. The addition of jam made the sandwich even more delicious and filling. My first jar of jam at Zellers cost seventy-five cents and lasted only a week.

Grocery shopping became the highlight of my week. I would spend at least a couple of hours going from aisle to aisle looking at the variety and wondering how one decided which jam and which peanut butter to buy when there were so many brands and versions. On weekends the store gave out samples of new products, such as soap or detergent. Sometimes they had snacks like olives or pickles, or cheese and crackers. I sampled everything so long as it was vegetarian. The food kept me full until dinner time. I had pickles, olives and Canadian Cheddar cheese for my first Christmas and New Year in Canada.

By late October, the weather had turned cold, and I was wearing all the clothes I had brought with me to stay warm. Coming from a tropical country, I had never seen snowflakes in my life and it fascinated me to see the heavy snowfalls which would sometimes last all day long. I was also in awe of the vapour coming out of my mouth when I spoke.

Another discovery I made was daylight saving time. I had never heard of such a concept prior to living in Canada. If I were to tell my Mauritian compatriots that we move our clock an hour back in the fall and then an hour forward in the spring, they would probably laugh and think I was trying to deceive them.

On the first morning after the time changed, I got up at my usual time for my 8:30 class on Monday morning. There were fewer people on the streets, but I did not think much of it. I was first to class, so I found my favourite seat and waited. Not one person arrived. I pulled out my timetable and checked it several times to ensure that there were no changes to the class time. After a few minutes, I decided to find Professor Adams and ask what was going on. He was not in his office.

I decided to see if Professor Frejer—whose office was at the other end of the campus, at least a good half kilometre—was in. He wasn't. Was school closed? I walked all the way back to Professor Adams' office and, out of ideas, sat down in the corridor. I can't remember how long I had been there, when I heard some footsteps coming in my direction. Professor Adams stood over me with a puzzled look. Was everything alright, he wanted to know.

I stood up. "No one is in class," I told him. "Was it cancelled?"

He frowned for a minute—then started to laugh. He invited me into his office, took off his coat, sat down on his chair, and looked at me with a strange kind of smile. "You forgot to turn your clock an hour back on Sunday morning. The professor did not cancel the class. It's only 7:50 a.m., not 8:50 a.m.. You are an hour early and no one is late."

I was so surprised that no words came out of my mouth.

"What?"

The idea seemed completely absurd, if not impossible. "Who decided that we move our clock an hour behind? Why was I not informed? Does everyone know about this?"

He tried to maintain his serious look, but I could tell that he found my response very funny. There was a knock on the door and he had to attend to one of his students. He sent me off to my psychology class and invited me to come back at the end of the day to continue our conversation.

Back at class, a few students were taking their seats. Feeling a sense of relief, I looked at the clock in the lecture hall. It was 9:20. I looked at my watch; it also said 9:20. I was puzzled. All day, the clock was the first thing that I would look at in each of my classes. Not one single clock had been set an hour early. I had a spare period that day so when I went to the library, I noticed that finally a clock was different and set to the appropriate new time.

I asked the person at the front desk why the clocks in Macdonald Hall were all set an hour late. She told me that the maintenance people did not get a chance to set all the clocks because they did not work on Sunday. But she assured me that all clocks on campus would be set to the right time by tomorrow morning so as not to create confusion for students. It takes a whole day to adjust the clocks, as there are hundreds of them on campus.

I thanked her, still only barely understanding the concept.

At the end of the day, Professor Adams was happy to explain it all. "Daylight saving time is a seasonal time change when the clocks are set an hour ahead of standard time. The change occurs in the spring and in the fall. In the spring we move our clock an hour forward and, in the fall, we move it an hour back. It is used to save energy and make better use of daylight. It was first used in 1908 in Thunder Bay, Canada."

"Who invented this?"

"I think it was invented by the New Zealand scientist George Vernon Hudson and the British builder William Willett in 1895. But it was only in 1908 that it caught the attention of the British Member of Parliament, Robert Pearce, who introduced a Bill to the House of Commons. It became law in 1916 and by that time, Willett had already died. Kind of sad that he may not have been aware that his idea became a reality. Daylight saving time is used in many countries; I can't tell you exactly how many. Next time you are in the library, look it up and let me know what you find."

*

When I no longer could bear the freezing cold walking to and from the university, I finally went to Zellers and bought my first winter coat. It was a short dark pink corduroy Sherpa jacket, on sale for ten dollars. I also bought two long-sleeved turtlenecks for another four dollars and a pair of gloves for twenty cents. I was happy to find clothes that fit my budget—but it was not really warm enough to take me through the winter months in Guelph. I kept my hands in my pockets and wore both turtlenecks underneath my jacket.

In my second semester, I enrolled in one of Professor Adams' African Literature courses. One day after class, when the snow was falling heavily on the ground and when everyone had left, Professor Adams approached me.

"I see you got a coat. It looks nice and light. You might need to get a scarf."

I had never heard of a scarf, so he drew one on the chalkboard and suggested that I pay attention to how other students wore theirs. He then told me that I was even allowed to try out the clothes in the store before buying them. If I changed my mind, I could always return items to the store for a full refund. I had never heard of anything like a refund policy, and it was quite a discovery. I did not return my pink corduroy jacket, even though it was not warm. It was my first jacket, and it was special. I finally bought a scarf in February—a grey one I found in the sale bin at Zellers. The scarf kept my neck and head warm when the temperature dipped to below -20°C, which was often.

Mrs. Estrada invited me to join her family for Christmas dinner, but I declined as I am a vegetarian and did not want to restrict or impose on their food choices. She was a single mother with a 10-year-old son. She was courteous, kind and quiet. She spoke Spanish and so we did not speak with one another very much. There was a side door that led to the basement. My room was next to the boiler and laundry room. We seldom crossed paths as she would do her laundry on Saturday morning when I was out for groceries, and when I was back around midday cooking in her kitchen, she would be gone.

Mrs. Estrada would bake cookies every Saturday afternoon. At first, she would offer me a glass of milk and a couple of her cookies for cleaning up her kitchen, my room and the common bathroom. But then I told her son, Nuno, that I am allergic to milk but would be happy to take her cookies. She gave me three cookies of various sorts every Saturday and I would keep them for my lunches.

One Saturday, I saw Mrs. Estrada coming home with a dozen jars of pasta sauce and a dozen cans of kidney beans. Shortly afterwards, I heard some noises from my room. She was trying to find room in the small cupboard by the boiler room. She told me that the pasta sauce and kidney beans were on sale at two for the price of one and that she bought her canned food when an item was on sale. She then asked me to follow her to the kitchen, where she showed me a pack of spaghetti. She told Nuno to explain to me that I could boil the spaghetti and eat it with the pasta sauce and kidney beans. I thanked her and, the next day, she offered me a bowl of cooked spaghetti with some pasta sauce for dinner. It was my first spaghetti meal and I liked it.

From that day, I would use spaghetti for noodles and fry them in oil, garlic and soy sauce for dinner. If the tomatoes were on sale, I would make a tomato salsa to accompany my garlic soy sauce noodles, just like Lan made them. Most of the time, I would eat the spaghetti noodles without the salsa.

I also did not understand why Mrs. Estrada would buy a dozen jars of pasta sauce at a time, as she would go for her groceries weekly. I later found out that her weekly menu was based on what was on sale. So, I tried to do the same to save money. I would eat spaghetti noodles for weeks before switching to fried rice, depending which was on sale. One time, I decided to buy five packs of spaghetti for one dollar instead of paying 23 cents per pack. The savings would allow me to get a can of mushrooms or a small jar of chilli flakes to add to my spaghetti sauce. I wrote to Lan and shared my newly found recipes and asked her for help to come up with menus for dinner and ingredients ideas. She had never heard of pasta sauce, but suggested that I could use diced tomatoes, garlic and onions to go with my spaghetti. In fact, I liked it much better than pasta sauce with spaghetti. I would sprinkle a few flakes of chilli on my tomato spaghetti.

Every Saturday I wrote to Mr. Chui and all the nuns about how my week went and to let them know how much I missed them. For the new year, I sent pictures of snowmen and a beautifully decorated Christmas tree that I had taken around the campus. They had only seen snow in postcards but, when they saw pictures of me posing with a snowman or near a Christmas tree, they were in awe. "Oh, no! You are so lucky," they would write, or "How does it feel to be near a real Christmas tree?"

In my second and final year, I had the late Professor Frejer for my advanced algebra and calculus courses. It was a big class of over two hundred students. I was average in math when I was in high school and did not like the subject much. I had to take math to fulfill my Bachelor of Arts requirements and decided to take the algebra course because it fit into my schedule. He was meticulous, well-organized, clear in his explanations and fair in his marking. He took interest in me because of my step-by-step explanations of Optimization, something I had learned in detail in high school and invited me to drop by his office for a quick chat.

My experience with teachers asking to see me had previously been negative. So, I almost had a panic attack. Instead of graciously accepting his invitation, I went up to him after the lecture and asked if he could speak with me then as I did not want to see him in his office. I could see from the expression on his face that he was quite taken aback and did not understand why I was obstinate. He insisted and I begrudgingly accepted to see him outside of class.

I duly went to his office the next day. He asked me what year I was in and when I told him that I was in my second and final year, he was surprised that on one hand I was still green to Canadian customs while on the other hand, I was taking advanced courses. He quizzed me about where I had developed such a passion for math. To his surprise, I told him that I was never very good in math; however, I am a logical person and so I like to put myself in the readers' shoes. I told him that when I think of math, I think of someone learning how to drive, as they need to be shown the basic skills such as the brake and the turn signals otherwise they end up crashing the car. Learning sequential math is just as important as learning how to drive. Therefore, mastering the order of operations is essential in mastering algebra. My answers to algebra problems reflect my understanding and mastering of the order of operations. He was pleased with my explanations and invited me to drop by during his office hours or when I had a spare period in my schedule.

I would visit Professor Frejer's office every other week for a few minutes, initially, and then the few minutes turned into an hour. We would talk about mathematics, philosophy, and the philosophers Descartes, Kant, Hume, Locke, and Popper. I would look them up and read about them to keep up with the conversation. For example, Professor Frejer asked me to look up Descartes, as he was famous for making the important connection between geometry and algebra, which allowed us to solve geometrical problems using algebraic equations.

As we got better acquainted, I shared how I felt reading Descartes' statement, "I think, therefore I am." This assurance had helped me feel secure in Mauritius, I told him, where there existed no records of my existence. This piqued his interest; I was far from the typical international Asian student he would normally have in his class. He asked me if I spoke Cantonese or Mandarin.

"Neither," I said. "But I speak four other languages: Hakka, English, French and Creole."

"We have a big population of Asian students from China, and I have quite a few of them in my course. The international Chinese students are very good in math and most of the time come up with the correct answer. But it is a challenge for them to give a step-by-step explanation of how they arrived at their answer," he said. "You have quite a facility for the English language, don't you?"

"English is not my mother tongue, although it is an official language in Mauritius. I spoke Hakka mixed with Creole in the pagoda and French and Creole at school."

The professor then admitted that he had never heard of Mauritius before and would look it up on a map. "Maybe I'll visit when I retire," he smiled.

"Yes, it is known as a paradise island. But I have yet to visit it myself."

"What do you mean, you have yet to visit the island?"

"Well, I would go from the temple to school and sometimes to my sponsor's store. That is all I have ever seen of Mauritius. I never ventured out past these places."

The professor asked to know more about me. "I am a founding member of this math department, founded in 1965. I want to know my students," he said.

I told Professor Frejer everything about my background and upbringing. As expected, he was surprised, telling me that I was courageous and smart. We ended the conversation when it was time to get to my next class. He invited me to drop by his office the next day and said that he would give me two books by Bertrand Russell, namely *Introduction to Mathematical Philosophy* and *Principles of Mathematics*.

*

In order to keep up with my studies, I had learned to be very efficient with other tasks. I did my shopping as fast as I could, then cooked and cleaned just as quickly. The goal was to return to the library. There, I would spend the weekend getting a head start on my assignments. I learned that I do not perform well under stress and so if I worked ahead and had all of my assignments completed and reviewed prior to the due dates, I felt much better. Both Professors Adams and Frejer would give me hints or tips, but they did not directly show me or steer me in any particular direction. Our conversations centred around solutions to mathematical problems, or colonialism, slavery, and religion. I enjoyed their company because they exposed me to different world views, and I had lots of time to think and even try out ideas.

Many years later, when I was promoted to head of a school, I wondered, "How do I balance the professional needs of my new teachers while at the same time optimizing students' learning under their care?" I revisited some of my conversations with Professor Frejer. He would tell us that "a mathematical statement is true if and only if it holds in any model of the axioms. Any statement is true if and only if it can be proven."

Likewise, when faced with the challenges of meeting the professional needs of my teachers, I read the works of Karl Popper and was intrigued by the possibilities of what his approach might mean for teachers' growth of knowledge. I wanted to use Popper's schema as a vehicle for teachers to recognize, articulate, communicate, and question their own knowledge and skills, and, in so doing, find the essence of what drives them as teachers. Through a sustained process of inquiry, reflection and communication, teachers can become avid learners of their own expertise. I have since managed to solve the generality/particularity problem and publish my research. These details are scattered throughout a hundred different papers. The gist is simple: defend the reliability of the epistemology as a process for constructing good theory, but let the resulting theories differ according to the prevailing contingencies, such as problems and resources, under which they were developed. Hence, there is no single best theory of educational leadership per se. Rather, a theory is best for a school given its circumstances, while another is best for another school given its different circumstances.

Professor Frejer paved the way for my thinking about these issues and for this I am grateful. He is thought of often and is missed.

After two full years, three semesters a year, I had one last elective course left to take to graduate. I decided that instead of living in Guelph, I would move to Toronto and commute. I applied for several entry-level clerical jobs and was offered one with an insurance company on Bloor Street. I learned that one of my professors, Professor Anderson, was commuting from Toronto three times a week. I enrolled in her course, "Perspectives of French Literature," and asked if it would be possible to catch a ride with her on those days. She agreed to charge me $3.00 for a return trip, which was much cheaper than taking the Greyhound.

As it turned out, she lived a couple of blocks away from my apartment on St. George Street. Every Wednesday morning, she would pick me up at 5:45 a.m. for our 8:30 a.m. class. Later in the day, we would leave Guelph around 2:30 p.m. to beat the rush hour traffic. While waiting for her, I would spend an hour reviewing my lecture notes or doing my assignment for the course and the rest of the time, would visit Professors Adams and Frejer. Now that I was spending much less time on campus, I was missing them. I wondered if my list of people whom I missed was longer than the people I knew. Wednesday became my favourite day of the week, as I got to ride in a luxury car with good company and good conversation.

I graduated from Guelph with a Bachelor of Arts degree, major in French and minor in Mathematics, with a cumulative average of 91% and a program average of 81.5%. I did not attend the graduation ceremony, as I had to work, and in any case, I had no family members or friends who would wish to attend the ceremony. Attending it would have been just another reminder of my humble beginnings.

A couple of months later, my degree and a cheque of $500 for being on the Dean's list came in the mail. I also received congratulations cards from both Professors Adams and Frejer. They asked me to keep in touch, and I did until I left to take a tenure track position at the University of Alabama in Huntsville. Professor Frejer passed away shortly after I left Canada.

To this day, I thank these professors for their guidance, conversations, compassion, and care. The famous

African proverb that says "It takes a village to raise a child" is fitting and appropriate, especially given that Professor Adams was of African descent and he kept an eye on me throughout my years in Guelph.

I am grateful to the village of people of various backgrounds who have shaped and contributed to the person I am today. In fact, research has also shown that when school, educators, parents, and the community work together, students get higher grades and attend school more regularly. In fact, the whole community has an essential role to play in the development of young adults. I am blessed to have had the community that I left backing me when I arrived in my adopted country.

Chapter 13

REUNITING

In 1987, after saving enough money working at the insurance company, I left my job for a holiday in Mauritius. I had many mixed feelings about this. Happy and excited, yes, but also worried that both myself and those I left behind had changed too much, that we would not recognize each other, and that Ah Pak would sense an even bigger distance between her and I.

Though I was barely making ends meet, I was determined to bring back a small token of appreciation for each of the nuns, as well as Mr. Chui and Mr. Alexander. I found a blue short-sleeved shirt with small pink flowers on sale for Mr. Chui. The shirt was well-made and was perfect for the tropical climate. I liked it so much and hoped he would wear it despite its femininity.

It was late July when I got on a plane again, returning a much different person. This time I had a degree, and my suitcase was full of gifts. I felt happy. Now it would be my turn to give back and show love and appreciation.

It was going smoothly until we landed at Charles de Gaulle. Shortly before our fight to Sir Seewoosagur Ramgoolam International Airport in Mauritius was set to leave, we were informed that there were mechanical problems and it would be delayed for another three hours. While waiting in the departure lounge, I overheard some conversations in Creole. I hesitated, then decided to strike up a conversation with some Mauritians. One of the women asked if I was studying in Paris and heading home for the summer. I told her that I had recently completed my bachelor's degree in Canada and that I was going to see my family. She was inquisitive, as most Mauritians are, and asked where my family lived. I did not want to get into telling my life story, so I gave her the address of the tea store and told her that my family lived on rue Léoville L'Homme. She asked if my family owned the tea store or if I knew the people who owned the store, as she knew Mr. Chui well. She and her brother went to the store every Thursday to buy tea to sell in their convenience store in Mahebourg. She asked me if Park was my brother, as she usually dealt with him. I just smiled and nodded yes.

It was almost midnight when we heard the announcement inviting all passengers for the flight to Mauritius to meet at the departure gate. But once there, we were told that the flight would not be leaving until the next day due to mechanical failure and that we would be given overnight accommodation at the Hilton Paris, with dinner and breakfast.

On the bus that took us to the Hilton, I caught a glimpse of Paris, a city I had heard so much about.

I was assigned a room on the seventh floor in a corner suite. The room was immaculate and the bathroom was fit for a queen. I had never stayed in a Hilton hotel before, and it felt like my first real vacation. I freshened up and went down to the restaurant to join the Mauritians for dinner.

There were at least three full banquet tables of them. I caught up with the latest news from Mauritius, the upcoming election, and the best hotels on the island. I still remember what I ordered: roasted beets with asparagus as an appetizer and wild mushroom risotto with melon sherbet to finish the meal. It was the best meal I ever had, and I am still thankful and grateful for it. Afterwards, back in my room, the bed was so soft and luxurious that I fell asleep immediately. It was a wonderful Parisian vacation.

The next day, we boarded the flight and landed safely, where I was met by Park and Ah Pak. There was a small delay at passport control, however, when they asked to see my return ticket. I did not exist in their database, so was technically a foreigner, a recent illegal migrant perhaps. I was reminded of the trouble Mr. Chui had to go through to get me re-entered into the country after I travelled with Ah Pak to Meixian. Finally, I got through.

I was in Mauritius for three weeks. I stayed with Ah Pak and got reacquainted with Lan's delicious meals, sweets, and savouries. This time, I paid more attention to how she made the smiling rice cake or the sesame balls stuffed with black beans that I loved so much, because I knew deep in my heart that I would not be returning to the pagoda for a long time. I visited the tea store every day to spend time with the Chuis, their employees, and the merchants. I also visited Mr. Alexander and Jane.

Strangely perhaps, reuniting with my moped made me happiest of all. Seeing it still waiting for me outside the kitchen remains one of the most memorable moments in my life. Every day I was in Mauritius, I helped Fen and Lan with their chores before heading out on my moped to the tea shop and staying as late as I could. Some days, I would have dinner with the Chuis. Most often, I would have lunch at the tea store then return to the pagoda for dinner. Riding through the village, even in my limited route, made me feel happy and that I belonged. It certainly helped to know that Ah Pak and Mr. Chui were proud of my accomplishments and who I had become.

The Chuis and the nuns found my story of the daylight saving time entertaining. When I told them how consumers can return merchandise for a full refund in Canada, even if it is only because they change their mind, they could not believe their ears. They asked if I had returned my winter jacket after I wore it. I told them that I did not, and Park looked disappointed and thought I should have returned it and exchanged it for a warmer jacket.

One night in the pagoda, we were all in Ah Pak's bedroom and it was getting late. I told them about my course with Professor Currie, who taught us that ghosts existed and that many of them had unfinished business and do not rest until it is communicated. Ah

Pak reminded us that on the night Jenny died, the drapes of the window in her room were moving and that I had been hallucinating. I asked her if she had heard any footsteps or knocks on the door or seen any ghost appearing and disappearing into thin air or going through walls. She said that some of us have more supernatural power than others and that although she was not a believer in the supernatural, on that night, she had been frightened by the drapes moving back and forth. We talked until we saw the sun rise and, while we were tired, I felt a sense of peace and acceptance. For the very first time in my life, I was not holding back my questions and was able to ask Ah Pak what I wanted.

After day broke, I helped Lan and Fen with all the chores before leaving for the tea store. I was free.

Chapter 14

PREMATURE

In 2002, the final year of my PhD studies, I was invited to give a talk at the University of Hong Kong. I decided to take the opportunity to learn more about my past.

Trudy was an intermediary for the visiting students at the University. I explained my story with as many details as I could manage. She took careful notes, made a few phone calls, and the next day arranged for me to speak with the gynecologist who delivered me. It took a few more days of intense negotiating with various hospital authorities, but then Trudy herself escorted me to the clinic to meet with Dr. Li. He was now in his late sixties or early seventies, and I worried that he could not possibly remember anything.

"How many babies have you delivered in your career," I asked, wanting to confirm my pessimism.

"In the thousands I would say," he said. "But I remember your birth. Well, not all of it. I recall your mother was a young woman in her late twenties. She was underweight, malnourished and had low blood pressure. You came in the world prematurely, around thirty-five weeks. At that time, we did not deliver many premature babies and so we did not know if you would make it or not. Your mother was afraid of losing you and begged us to do everything possible to save your life. You were my first premature baby, in fact. I was quite apprehensive. You had to stay in the clinic for a week before you were discharged."

"But how can you be sure that was me?" I was starting to think this visit was fruitless and he was just weaving tales for both of our satisfactions.

He thought for a minute. "You have a birthmark in the upper middle of your back. It looks like a fly. Am I correct?"

I felt the blood leave my face for a moment, as if seeing a ghost. My past, my history, a phantom for so long. "Yes, you are correct."

"You were frail and small in weight," he continued. "Less than four pounds. Your mother was not lactating and so you had to be fed by bottles every two hours. "Where was my mother?" The nurses fed you on shifts."

"Hmm," he said. "That I don't know. I don't think I was the doctor who discharged you."

"Who discharged me? And who came to pick me up?" Surely the story cannot end here, I thought. He must have more.

"I don't have this information," he said. I could tell that my desperation was wearing on him. "It was decades ago, and I don't think we have the information you are asking. I remember you because you were the first premature baby I delivered and so, like I said, I was apprehensive for both the mother and the baby."

PREMATURE

My birth was a medical story for him, an accomplishment, a professional experience and a skill that he would build on. I should not have resented that, but I did.

Chapter 15

A DREAM

It was July 2011, and I was teaching an intensive summer course on a very hot day. After class, I went home and took a nap in the middle of the afternoon. Falling into a deep sleep, I had an odd and mysterious dream, which left me feeling deeply disturbed when I awoke. It was vivid and aroused strong feeling of sadness. It felt like a message.

In the dream, I was vacationing in Mauritius and Ah Pak told me I should visit Mr. Chui, as he was ill. When I got to the tea store, Park and Shu pointed me upstairs where he was resting in his room. I found him standing at the sink next to his bedroom, washing up. He did not know I was there, and I pretended I did not see him, as he was unclothed. Once I saw his bare back, I walked the other way and waited for him to be clothed. Once he was back in his bed, I went in. I knelt and put my arms around his neck and told him that I loved him very much and asked him to please tell me who my parents were.

He did not answer. I asked if he had promised my parents that he would never reveal who they are to me. The silence and knowing this may have been my last chance to discover who my parents were made me cry uncontrollably. I told him that I missed him very much and that I would come back to visit him from time to time. When I stood up, I saw the last picture of Mr. Chui, taken just before he passed, hanging on the wall. In that picture, he was wearing light blue pyjamas, sitting in his walker. Somehow, the picture reminded me that he was dead. I woke up awash in tears.

It was almost midnight, Mauritian time, when I decided to ring Park up and tell him about my dream. I asked him when was the last time that he visited his father's tomb in Nam Soon Cemetery, and also when was the last time he paid a visit to his father's tablet which was housed in one of the buildings in the pagoda.

Park was not ready for this line of questioning. "I don't know. Do you know what time it is? You scared me with this late-night phone call. Is everything alright?"

I was impatient. "Yes, everything is fine. I dreamt of your dad. I think he is in trouble."

"What do you mean he is in trouble?" A fair question considering that Mr. Chui had been dead for two decades.

"I dreamt of him standing by the sink next to his bedroom, naked. I haven't been a practicing Buddhist since I left but, seeing someone all naked is not a good sign."

"I agree, but what do you want me to do?"

"It can mean lots of things such as, he is going through a hard time. Can you go to the pagoda and burn some paper votives for him?"

Ah Pak and Koung Koung had taught me that in the Chinese Buddhism and folk traditions, when deceased relatives come into your dream, it usually means that they are communicating their needs to the living. Since I found Mr. Chui naked, the first thought that came to mind was that he had given away his last piece of clothing and he needed money to buy new clothes. I also asked Park to speak with Ah Pak and to tell her about my dream.

He got back to me a few days later and told me that he went to the pagoda and did as I had asked. I felt a sense of relief.

But in 2013, I was informed by Park and Hu that the tea store would be closing its doors for good, after they sold their last carton, as Bois Chéri had found another distributor for their tea. I was heartbroken.

To this day, when I think of the dream, I think of it as a Mystery, and I don't know what it means. I have read many mysteries and understood that when something is a mystery, it is because the solution has not yet been found. But mystery and Mystery are two different things. Rachel Ramen (2000) a physician and counsellor of chronic and terminal illness, once said, "By its very nature, a Mystery cannot be solved; it can never be known. It can only be lived."[3]

---

3. Rachel Ramen, *My Grandfather's Blessings: Stories of Strength, Refuge, and Belonging.* New York: Riverhead Books, p. 337.

Even though I grew up in a Buddhist temple, I was not raised to cultivate a sense of Mystery. As an academic, I sometimes see Mystery or the unknown as an insult to my competence or a personal failing. When I view Mystery in that sense, it becomes a challenge to action. Perhaps the Mystery of my dream requires that I pay attention and be open to possibilities.

In the temple, I saw how Mystery comforted worshippers when nothing else worked. I saw Mystery heal sicknesses that were otherwise unhealable. I witnessed worshippers recover from cancer and go on to live for many years. There is a dimension of the unknown in everything and everyone. Mystery can speak to us and heal us, and it allows us to listen to life. Perhaps real wisdom lies in not seeking answers to the unknown because any answer that I find about my dream will only hold true temporarily, just to help me fall asleep as life moves past me to its next question. Many years have passed, and I began to wonder if the secret of living well is not about finding answers but continuing to pursue unanswerable questions with like-minded people.

My dream of Mr. Chui offers neither proof nor certainty that he was in trouble. Perhaps, it is just a reminder for me to stay awake, listen and be present, because the Mystery at the heart of life can speak to us at any time.

I was first introduced to the work of Dr. Ramen by my son, Jeremy, who was studying to become a psychiatrist. I was moved by her compassion, altruism and service, among other qualities of a physician. Rachel

Ramen recounted experiences, told to her by many fellow physicians, that could not be explained but which had changed them or caused them to wonder.

Like the physicians, Mystery came to occupy a central place in my life. Things happen that science cannot explain; important things that cannot be measured but can only be observed, witnessed, known or felt. Most of all they are not replicable, generalizable and they cannot be corroborated.

I welcome those moments when I dream of Mr. Chui. I do not go to bed thinking about him or telling myself that I want to dream of him. It just happens more often than anticipated. I used to protect myself from losses, and the deaths of loved ones are most certainly losses. At the beginning, I did not allow myself to be touched by life or to participate in it. I later realized that the many strategies that I had used to shelter myself from feeling loss do not lead to healing. When Mr. Chui passed, I used denial, rationalization, substitution, and avoidance to numb the pain of loss, and every one of these strategies hurt me in some far more fundamental ways. None of them were respectful of life or the life process, and none of them acknowledged my capacity to find meaning or wisdom. It was only through months of therapy and grieving that I was able to heal, and this allowed me to participate fully in life.

I was fortunate to be introduced to Michelle, a middle-aged therapist. I looked forward to my sessions with her, as she provided me with a safe environment in which to heal. Gradually, she helped me transform the suffering of my losses into wisdom. It started with the realization that my losses have become a part of me and have altered my life so profoundly that I cannot go back to the way it was before. She said once, "In the face of all your sufferings, all I want to do is to bear witness so that you do not have to suffer alone." More than anything, this validated my worth as a human being.

It was a sorting process. At the beginning, I experienced everything; then, gradually, I let go one by one—the anger of losing both Mr. Chui and Koung Koung in the same year; the guilt and shame of not being able to attend their funerals; and the anger that Pow Koung, the God of Justice, had taken away from me the very people I loved the most. Where is the justice in that?

But one day, even the pain itself left, and all I had left was a deep sense of the value of life and a greater capacity to live it.

Mr. Chui and Ah Pak believed that their first responsibility to an unwanted child was to protect her. Because they cared deeply about people, it made them vulnerable. They exposed and involved themselves, which came with risks, processes, and criticisms. They wanted to make a difference and making a difference required they face disappointment, loss and even ridicule. They believed that giving the right protection was something within them rather than something between them and the world. Perhaps, if more people were like Mr. Chui and Ah Pak, it would strengthen our capacity to repair the world. It is easy to forget that every life matters and that each one of us is worthy of unconditional love. Mr. Chui and Ah Pak each believed that human actions help to move things in the direction that Buddha wants them to move, to free them from suffering. Because they were both leaders, they have the same dream that Buddha has.

Somehow, both Ah Pak and Mr. Chui understood that few of us are ever truly free. Recognition, money, power, success, beauty; whatever we are attached to will enslave us and often we inadvertently become their slaves. I am conscious of the many things that enslave us and limit our ability to live fully and that might even cause suffering. Freedom represents freedom from hunger or fear, from discrimination against my socioeconomic status or the colour of my skin, or from injustice. Perhaps freedom at the deepest level is the same for us all, that is, the capacity to know and live by the innate goodness in us, to give, serve and belong to each other, as Mr. Chui, Ah Pak and all the people in the book have done.

To this day, my heart is filled with loving memories of my relationship with both Mr. Chui and Ah Pak.

Epilogue

THE RETURN

It is April Fool's Day, a date in Canada where we are warned not to take anything too seriously. So, when I get news that a research project has been awarded full funding, I wonder who is playing this joke on me. This is not just any project, but one that will take me back to Mauritius—this time for an extended period and allow me to finally get to the bottom of some issues and secrets in my history.

The next day the offer still stands and I buy our tickets. One of my sons will accompany me. After a whirlwind of planning and organizing, we land in Mauritius in the early morning of May 13, 2022. I have booked us a nice hotel and we check in for a much-needed rest. Justin is beyond exhausted and unwilling to do anything before sleeping a full eight hours. I am unable to rest for a long time. It is not my scholarly research that weighs heavily on me, but challenges of a more personal nature. What I want is simple, but how I might have to go about getting it is very complicated.

The next morning, I prepare to pay my respects to the two women who raised me. Cemeteries are dangerous places in Mauritius, often inhabited by thieves ready to rob the expats who return to pay their respects to family members. However, thanks to the generosity of Vincent MacDonald and his wife Valerie, two officers are to accompany us to the two cemeteries where Ah Pak and Koung Koung are resting. The agents meet us in the lobby. I feel safe with these two taciturn men at our sides.

Our first stop is the Bois Marchand cemetery. Koung Koung passed in 1989, some three decades ago. The few occasions when I returned in the past, I had asked the nuns at Fook Soo Am if we could visit her resting place, but they discouraged me from going to the cemetery due to the danger. Instead, we prayed at the pagoda in front of her picture.

This time, protected by our "bodyguards," we make our way towards the section of the cemetery where the tombs are shaped like pagodas. I read the names on all of them, but never see hers. Finally, either out of compassion or overheating, one of the officers asks a passing gardien if he might know where a Buddhist nun could be buried. The gardien walked us to a freshly painted structure that I did not recognize. It is Koung Koung's tomb.

I have incense in my bag and my son helps me light it. We also burn Canadian paper money and make an offering of food that she used to love—dried goji berries, ginger candies, dried Shitake mushrooms, dried lotus seeds, and chrysanthemum tea. This food has travelled with us from Ottawa. I climb up on her tomb and touch a picture of her etched on the marble. I begin to pray. It is not really a prayer, but just a conversation in my head. I need to talk to her.

I wonder if she remembers me. It has been so long since I visited. I motion to my son, introduce him to her in my head. His name is Justin, and I almost apologize. It is not a Chinese name, and I hope she doesn't find that strange. But he is doing his PhD in bioinformatics—another strange thing, I am sure. My other son, Jeremy, is also accomplished, I tell her: he is an Assistant Professor of Psychiatry at the The Schulich School of Medicine, University of Western Ontario, and a Psychiatrist at the First Episode Mood and Anxiety Program (FEMAP) in London, Ontario.

In my hand is a bag: I bought you some goji berries which are good for your eyes, I said, and ginger candies and lotus seeds which you used to love. I continue to live by all your teachings, be good, kind and compassionate towards all people regardless of race, gender or status in life. Continue to watch over us and I will visit you again before I leave for Ottawa. I love you.

Have I been speaking out loud? I am not sure. My son catches me as I climbed down. Together we bow and I give Koung Koung a long hug by crisscrossing my arms.

Our next stop is Nam Soon cemetery where Ah Pak has been resting since September 14, 2021. It seems that Samuel, one of the officers, knows where Ah Pak's tomb is, and they let us off nearby. A gardien is there and he points just to the left of us. Like Koung Koung's, it is a small pagoda with her portrait etched in the stone. I am overcome with emotion and begin to cry, my absence during her last days and death weighing heavily on me.

In the last months of Ah Pak's life, I had dreams where I fell and floated in endless darkness. There was no up or down in this vast and dark space, and I was utterly alone. I associated this feeling with Ah Pak, her absence and the distance between us, and eventually went to bed anticipating these dreams and its liminal state where I knew she was close. She eventually appeared. We'd be sitting on a bench in a public garden, perhaps in Caudan, Port Louis, surrounded by beautiful flowers. I told Ah Pak that the nuns were scolding me and prohibiting me from visiting. The nuns were being mean to me, I told her. I woke up to a soaking wet pillow.

When the news of her death had reached me—not directly from the nuns at the pagoda, but from one of Mr. Chui's granddaughters—I tried to book a flight for the funeral but getting a PCR test in time proved to be impossible. I went to the travel clinic but missed the closing hours by only a few minutes. I called around to pharmacies and managed to get an appointment.

However, Mauritius required all passengers to present a negative PCR test taken within 72 hours before departure—a timeline that proved impossible.

I reached out to Mr. Chui's family and asked if they could have some influence with the nuns and asked that the funeral be delayed. But the nuns were not amenable for several reasons.

They did not want the body to wait in a morgue for me, a technicality that I knew was irrelevant. More importantly, they did not see me as family or even community. Upon hearing this, I was shocked beyond belief.

The fall semester had just started the week before and I was teaching two graduate online courses. I plunged into a grief so profound and immobilizing that I had to take a personal leave of absence for several weeks. While on leave, I realized that I had put off returning since 2017 because one of the nuns had told me that I had broken Ah Pak's heart all those years ago, and therefore must stop visiting. I did not put too much weight on that conversation at the time, as they hadn't prevented me from showing up. Until then, I had been returning to Mauritius and visiting Ah Pak every couple of years. In 2013, I brought my sons, whom she enjoyed and spoiled. I could see, however, her diminished role at the pagoda and the increasing control of the nuns—not all of it positive or in her best interests.

My last visit in 2017 was supervised by the nuns, but Ah Pak managed to tell me three things quietly and discretely: (i) "I have no power—*Gaye more kien*"; (ii) "I rely on them to be fed—*Oy qui ten yin na gaye set*"; (iii) "I have signed some papers having to do with the Pagoda—*Qui ten yin va gaye zor ti poune ki*."

Before the end of that last visit, one of the nuns told me that she did not understand why I needed to keep coming back to the pagoda. The young wards, as well, were asking why, as an ex-ward, I should be allowed to visit. They saw me as someone who had disobeyed Ah Pak and broken her heart yet dared to return. I was not good for her, they told me. Stay away, they repeatedly said. After that, they declined my subsequent requests to see her. When I left Mauritius in 2017, I vowed to return in a couple of years. But then came Covid.

After Ah Pak's death, I did some digging and learned that she had donated the pagoda to an Association. Consisting of nuns, the Association gave its members the authority to run the day-to-day operations. This explained even more why I was not welcome: the nuns likely saw me as, at best, an interloper, and at worst, a threat to their authority and ownership.

I touch the stones of Ah Pak's tomb and want her to know I am sorry that I did not take any actions or investigate all this before her death, but I did not want to cause any problems or motivate them to mistreat her. I was powerless and far away and had my own life to manage. On the surface, it appeared that she was well looked after by the nuns and, to be honest, I did not want to think otherwise.

I put the dried food in a plastic bag and burn more paper money. The whole ceremony lasts about half an hour. I am light-headed and completely drained of energy yet buzzing as if an entire flock of birds has taken residence in my body. The officers open the car doors and Justin and I get inside. There is still somewhere else I must go.

When we arrive at the pagoda, I am overcome with emotion and tears stream down my cheeks. It is my first time visiting since Ah Pak's death. Despite that, I am looking forward to seeing my favourite god, Pow Koung. I ring the doorbells several times but there is no answer. Samuel calls the pagoda's number and it picks up.

"Ena enn dam ki sorti Canada qui oule rant dan Pagod," he says in Creole. *There is a woman from Canada who wants to come in.*

He puts his phone on speaker and I can hear the nun clearly: "Madam ki? Madam ki Madam Canada pe rode napas la ek legliz finn ferme." *What woman? The woman that the Canada woman wants to see is no longer here. And the pagoda is closed.*

"Les mwa pas telefonn Madam Canada la," Samuel says. *Let me pass the phone to the woman from Canada.* But the nun hangs up.

I cannot say anything for several minutes. I am heartbroken, flabbergasted, even embarrassed. This is the home of my childhood, of Ah Pak's dedication and vocation, of all our service. The pagoda is a public place and never in my entire time growing up there did I know us to turn people away. I know the nuns who are there now and while they may be suspicious of me, I do not understand this blanket hostility. I thank Samuel for his interventions, and we drive back to the hotel.

Days pass and I am getting more and more agitated and helpless. I am unable to find out anything about Ah Pak. How and where she died? How were her final hours? What was the cause of her death? These questions nag me and burn my insides. I am determined to find out what I can on my own.

I visit the Birth and Death Certificate Offices in Port Louis. It is a frustrating and infuriating process, but after two days I finally manage to obtain her death certificate. No cause of death is recorded, however. In other papers I see the name of a Mr. Ryan who had overseen the pagoda's affairs, and once again find myself seeking the assistance of Mr. Vincent MacDonald to connect me. After several attempts, Mr. Ryan finally returns Vincent's calls and agrees to see me the following day.

I travel to a small office building in Phoenix, a town in the interior of the island. A woman greets me and motions me to the lounge. Ten minutes later, Mr. Ryan ushers me into his office and sits across from me at a large table. I thank him for meeting me on such short notice and for such an odd request. I explain that I am in Mauritius on a research assignment and do not have much time. I explain my visits to the cemetery and a little bit about my life at the pagoda.

"I just do not understand why I am not being given any information about Ah Pak's final circumstances," I say. "I am practically her daughter. She was effectively my mother. I don't know how she died, how were her final hours, or even the cause of her death."

Ryan nods with some compassion. He might not have all the answers, but he has some, he says. "Ah Pak had some skin problem, a kind of dermatitis, on her hands which then it moved to her head. Then one day she fell and after her fall she was bedridden for a while." He takes a long pause. "I did not know about you."

The simplicity of his answer, however, does not fill in all the gaps.

"You have parents," I say, suddenly feeling bold and righteous. "How would you feel if your parents were ill or died and no one told you and your concerns were dismissed?"

"I am very sorry. No one told me about you," he repeats. "My mother used to go to the Pagoda and knew Ah Pak well. When my mother passed, I continued to visit the pagoda in her name. Ah Pak always prayed for me and my family."

"Can you explain why the nuns do not allow me entry?"

He seems genuinely puzzled. "I am surprised. The pagoda is a public place. As for overseeing the pagoda's affairs, it is barely personal. I give money and send workers and gardeners to help in its maintenance. But to be honest, I am just not there very often. I do not know the nuns well or the details of their dealings with people."

I try another approach. "Do you know the doctors who treated Ah Pak?"

He thinks for a few seconds. "I believe it was Dr. Smith. Let me give him a call and see if he can meet with you."

There is no more to say. I thank Mr. Ryan and he walks me to the car. I am on my way to the hotel when I receive a text from him. He has found Ah Pak's death certificate. But it is a replica of what I already have: a document with the date of her death, but no cause. While it does not advance my search, it is reassuring to know he is helping me. He then sends me a text asking if I would meet the daughter of Ah Pak to clear the air. This is immediately followed by another text: "Sorry, that message was not for you. It was for the doctor."

Given the incomprehensible roadblocks I am facing in this otherwise banal quest—to visit my childhood home and know more about the final days of Ah Pak—I am suspicious enough to hold on to the message and take it as a sign of further intrigue. I don't know if I'm being savvy or ridiculous.

The next day, I call up Dr. Smith. I explain who I am and ask to know more about the cause of her death.

"She had a fall and had a concussion and from there she was in a vegetative state. She needed to be fed, bathed and cared for, which the nuns did," he says. This is a plausible story, though slightly different from the one Mr. Ryan told me.

"May I see a cause of death certificate?" I ask.

"I am not sure I can give it to you." He does not know who I am, he explains. Also, he would need permission from the nuns for this. "Let me talk to the nuns and get back to you tomorrow."

He texts me the next day, this time saying that he cannot confirm if Ah Pak passed at home or at the clinic "as I did not see her."

This does not make sense to me—why did he say he needed the nuns' permission to give me the certificate if he did not see her or have any useful information to share?

I leave a message for Mr. Ryan asking if he can facilitate my entrance to the pagoda as he is highly respected by the nuns. He does not return my calls.

A few days later, however, I make some headway. With the help of a few members of the business community who knew Ah Pak, the nuns are obliged to allow me to enter. I can retrieve a few of Ah Pak's items, including a pair of black earrings that I bought her with my first paycheck. I also find a document she had left for me. A clairvoyant had visited the pagoda years ago, offering her services in exchange for a meal. Ah Pak accepted, and had the woman do a reading of my life. I did not read it then and may never read it. I realize what it actually is: more evidence that I was loved and that my future was of some concern to someone. I tuck it in my bag.

Before leaving, I press the nuns for more details of Ah Pak's illness and final days, but they are vague. I realize that every person who was linked to her death claims not to have seen a Cause of Death certificate. It is a mystery. It might even be a Mystery.

I leave Mauritius no wiser, but somewhat more able to move on. I decide that I don't want to wander in bondage in the fog surrounding her death. I don't want to be immobilized by desire or greed or constrained by notions of victimhood or entitlement. I don't want to cling to places and behaviour that are small, petty and hurtful. I can't resent the nuns any longer. I have to let go.

I return with a photograph of Ah Pak, which I frame and hang in my home office. For the first time, it feels like I have brought her back home to live with me. She is now more than just a person from my past; for the very first time she is part of my future.

ACKNOWLEDGEMENTS

In 2021, I created a scholarship at the University of Ottawa in Ah Pak's name: the Ah Feeti of Fook Soo Am Memorial Scholarship. Through this I hope to help racialized students, including Indigenous, Métis and Inuit, who are pursuing undergraduate degrees in the Faculty of Education. I do this in memory of her, and to honour my own long struggle. Very little in this life is easy, I know that all too well. But also, very little is impossible, and for that I thank Ah Pak, Koung Koung, Mr. Chui, Marvin Zuker, Professors Adams and Frejer, and everyone else who helped me stay standing and moving forward.

This memoir began as a need to acknowledge my existence and to share with my readers the words of my mentors, friends and guardians—words that have stayed with me throughout this spiritual and spirited journey. It is for this reason that I have chosen to commit my journey onto the pages of this book.

Blessings to Ah Pak for her courage in raising me, for mustering divine strength in the face of adversity and for putting up with my mouthiness. I have never doubted the mutual love and respect that we have between us, despite the physical distance.

Blessings to Koung Koung for making me feel that I was already enough when I struggled to learn and to know more and when it was never good enough. You were gone too soon but are never far from my thoughts.

Blessings to the late Mr. Chui for fostering my independence and for encouraging me to broaden my horizons beyond the temple and beyond Mauritius Island. He was my hero and had taught me so many things such as to never let anyone talk down to me and for reminding me, often, that I can do anything I want. Thank you for all the love that will last me a lifetime.

Blessings to the worshippers at the pagoda. "Fook Soo Am" for your kindness, generosity and nourishment.

Blessings to everyone who has contributed to shaping me into the person I am today. You will know who you are in the story, even though I have given you different names.

Blessings to the late Professors Adams and Frejer for their support and compassion. Thanks to you, I endeavour to play a similar role for my students, present and future.

Blessings to Leila Marshy, my editor and at times even co-writer, for being simply the best and for her encouraging feedback during this process. It was indispensable.

Blessings to Marc Brassard writing the captions of the photographs and for introducing me to François Couture.

Blessings to François Couture for believing in my work and for his encouraging feedback during the writing process.

ACKNOWLEDGEMENTS

Heartfelt blessings to Philip Ah Chuen, educator, and philanthropist, who I had the pleasure to meet last May when I was searching for a publisher in Mauritius.

A special blessing to Professor Cecile Leung for reading every word and providing me with valuable feedback. I am grateful for her foreword which depicts well my trajectory.

Blessings to Dean and Professor Arnaud Carpooran of the Faculty of Social Sciences at the University of Mauritius for your inspiring words and for reminding me to continue practicing my Creole.

Blessings to Professor and Dean Richard Barwell of the Faculty of Education at the University of Ottawa. I greatly appreciate your support and optimism regarding this manuscript. And for reminding me to take time for myself. It has been a privilege to work with you as you are one of a kind.

Blessings to Blossom Thom , Anne Marie Marko and Daniel J. Rowe for reading from the very beginning, generously, and for believing.

I would like to thank the readers of my previous books for their support, which means so much to me.

In addition, I would like to thank Robin Philpot, the publisher for believing in my story: otherwise it would have never seen the light of day.

Finally, blessings to my sons Justin, Jeremy, his wife Colleen, and my granddaughter, Juniper for all their love.

All proceeds from the sales of this book goes to Ah Feeti of Fook Soo Am Memorial Scholarship.

REFERENCES

Albom, M. 1997. *Tuesdays with Morrie*. New York: Doubleday.

Remen, R. N. 2000. *My Grandfather's Blessings: Stories of Strength, Refuge, and Belonging*. New York: Riverhead Books.

ABOUT THE AUTHOR

Dr. Stephanie Chitpin is a Full Professor of Leadership at the Faculty of Education, University of Ottawa, where she received the 2020 Research Excellence Award. Her research is international in scope. Author of over 100 articles and several books on leadership and professional development of educators, she founded the Equitable Leadership Network and is Series Editor of *Transforming Education Through Critical Leadership, Policy and Practice*. Stephanie Chitpin lives in Ottawa, Canada.

ALSO FROM BARAKA BOOKS

ᐧᐊᔅᐧᐊᓂᐲ Waswanipi
Jean-Yves Soucy
with an Afterword by Romeo Saganash

Stolen Motherhood
Surrogacy and Made-to-Order Children
Maria De Koninck

Still Crying for Help
The Failure of Our Mental Healthcare Services
Sadia Messaili

Mussolini Also Did a Lot of Good
The Spread of Historical Amnesia
Francesco Filippi

A Distinct Alien Race
The Untold Story of Franco-Americans
David Vermette

Montreal and the Bomb
Gilles Sabourin

After All Was Lost
The Resilience of a Rwandan Family Orphaned on April 6, 1994
when the Rwandan President's Plane was Shot Down
Alice Nsabimana (June 2023)

The Legacy of Louis Riel
Leader of the Métis People
John Andrew Morrow (June 2023)

The Einstein File
The FBI's Secret War on the World's Most Famous Scientist
Fred Jerome